MS.
The Story of Gloria Steinem

MS.
The Story of Gloria Steinem

Elizabeth Wheaton

620 South Elm Street, Suite 223
Greensboro, North Carolina   27406
http://www.morganreynolds.com

MS.: THE STORY OF GLORIA STEINEM

Copyright © 2002 by Elizabeth Wheaton

Cover photo of Gloria Steinem © AP Photo/Robert F. Bukaty.

Library of Congress Cataloging-in-Publication Data

Wheaton, Elizabeth.
    MS : the story of Gloria Steinem / Elizabeth Wheaton.
        p. cm.
    Includes bibliographical references and index.
    Summary: A biography of the feminist writer and activist, founder of Ms. magazine and
    the Ms. Foundation, and her impact on the women's movement.
    ISBN 1-883846-82-X (lib. bdg.)
        1. Steinem, Gloria--Juvenile literature. 2. Feminists--United
    States--Biography--Juvenile literature. 3. Ms--Juvenile literature. [1. Steinem, Gloria. 2.
    Feminists. 3. Women--Biography.] I. Title.

HQ1413.S645 W48 2001
305.42'092--dc21
[B]
                                                                    2001040204

Printed in the United States of America
First Edition

In memory of my brother and lifelong friend
Stuart Thomas Ege

With special thanks to
Barbara Leary, for reminding me of my feminist *clumps*;
and Gloria Steinem, for sharing her inner voice.

Contents

Chapter One

Heritage 9

Chapter Two

A Child's Worst Fears 16

Chapter Three

Independence 24

Chapter Four

Writer and Activist 31

Chapter Five

Awakening 40

Chapter Six

The Road to Feminism 47

Chapter Seven

Breakthrough 53

Chapter Eight

Call Me *Ms.* 61

Chapter Nine

CLICK! 74

Chapter Ten

Trashing 82

Chapter Eleven

Revolution from Within 91

Sources 100

Bibliography 107

Index 110

Gloria Steinem *(AP Photo/Robert F. Bukaty)*

Chapter One

Heritage

In 1983, Gloria Steinem dedicated her book *Outrageous Acts and Everyday Rebellions* to her father, Leo, "who taught me to love and live with insecurity," and to her mother, Ruth, "who performed the miracle of loving others even when she could not love herself." While Gloria's childhood was marred by Leo's absence and Ruth's mental illness, their abiding love infused her with strength, devotion, and compassion.

Ruth and Leo met in Toledo, Ohio. Ruth's mother, Marie Ochs Nuneviller, had been a teacher before marrying Gloria's grandfather. Marie was stern, ambitious, and demanding. When it came time to wean little Ruth, Marie took her to a friend's house and left her there until the child was accustomed to drinking from a bottle or a cup. Throughout her childhood, Ruth was often left alone. Her mother would not tell her where she was going or when she would return.

Marie also held high ambitions for her daughter and lectured her on the importance of going to a "good" college and becoming a teacher, one of the few acceptable careers for women at the time. Marie insisted that Ruth have a profession. Ruth grew to be an independent and spirited teen, playing basketball and startling neighbors by wearing her father's overalls to work in the garden.

In 1916, Ruth entered Oberlin College and discovered her passion for writing. She had always been an avid reader, and she blossomed in the free-thinking atmosphere of the small college. Her dream was to go to New York City to become a newspaper writer. It was not long, though, before Marie's savings ran out and Ruth had to leave Oberlin and return home, get a part-time job, and attend the University of Toledo. There she met Leo Steinem, the editor of the campus newspaper. He recruited Ruth to work with him, and soon she found herself falling in love—with newspaper writing as well as with Leo.

In Leo, Ruth found a zany, devil-may-care fellow who did not give a whit about graduating. He was a gifted salesman, and among the things he sold best were his dreams for a grand future. He was also a gentle and lovingly demonstrative man, just about as unlike Ruth's mother as a person could be.

Both families were opposed to the relationship—the Nunevillers because Leo was Jewish, the Steinems because Ruth was not. But they married secretly while in college. Then in 1921, when both families had become accustomed to the idea, they had a public marriage ceremony.

It did not take Ruth long to become close to Leo's

Gloria's parents, Ruth and Leo Steinem, met at the University of Toledo, where they were both students, in 1919. *(University of Toledo Archives)*

mother, Pauline. Unlike Marie, Pauline was open and generous; like Ruth, she was a free-thinker and a bit of a rebel. Pauline was a feminist who organized women's groups, worked for women's suffrage, and even testified before Congress. In 1908, she was one of two American delegates to attend the International Council on Women in Switzerland.

Pauline's independent streak extended to her religious beliefs. She became deeply involved with Theosophy, a belief system that flourished in the mid-to-late nineteenth century. The word *theosophy* means "divine wisdom." Its followers believe in the essential oneness of all living things; altruism and compassion are guiding principles. The American Theosophical Society, still active today, explains further: "We are responsible for our own lives. No one else—divine or human—can take away or neutralize the results of any of our actions."

Ruth and Pauline spent hours talking and reading about Theosophy, and Ruth passed her knowledge on to her daughters. Gloria has called Ruth's beliefs one of her "most important inheritances."

As Leo began pursuing his business ventures, Ruth returned to the University of Toledo to get her master's degree and—as her mother had insisted all along—her teaching certificate. Leo's business ventures began to pay off, and with his father's help he built a house on the Maumee River in Toledo.

Ruth got a job writing a gossip column for a small weekly paper, though she had to write under a male pen name. It did not take long for the daily *Toledo Blade* to take notice, and she was soon offered a job as their society columnist under her own name. Just prior to Susanne's birth on February 19, 1925, Ruth was made editor of the Sunday edition of the paper—"the best-paid job on the paper for any employee, male or female," Ruth later told Gloria.

Life was grand for the Steinems: A full-time house-keeper, private school for Susanne, and clothes from the finest shops in Toledo. In 1928, Leo built a summer resort at Clark Lake, Michigan, about fifty miles north-west of Toledo. He brought in top musicians and drew crowds from Detroit as well as Toledo. His goal, Gloria later said, was to have "a resort worthy of the big dance bands of the '30s." Their first year's income—$50,000—was a fortune at the time.

But their storybook life did not last. Ruth quit her editorial post to help Leo run the resort. She became pregnant again, but one day she began bleeding and asked her mother to call a doctor. Characteristically, Marie had her own ideas about what was happening. She believed that Ruth was exaggerating and thus refused to get help, and Ruth suffered a miscarriage.

The stock market crash of October 1929 spiraled into the Great Depression, and Leo's business ventures began to fail. The family had to sell their dream home, and in 1930 they moved permanently to Clark Lake, where they could live more cheaply. To earn income when the resort closed for the winter, Leo began buying antiques at rural auctions and trying to sell them for a profit in the cities, where some people still had extra cash for luxuries.

Though Leo was making enough to support the family, he traveled for days at a time, leaving Ruth alone with Susanne. Clark Lake was several miles from the nearest town. The isolation was agony for Ruth, who was often anxious and afraid. Then one summer day a boy was killed in an accident at the lake, and Ruth's anxiety turned to terror. She began to hear awful noises in the wind and finally suffered a complete breakdown. After spending several months in a sanitarium in Toledo, Ruth returned to the lake. But she was never the same again.

On March 25, 1934, nine years after Susanne was born, Ruth Steinem gave birth to a baby girl at a hospital in Toledo. (Ruth was not about to risk losing another baby by remaining alone at the lake.) Susanne had been so eager for a baby sister that Ruth and Leo allowed her to pick the child's name. Susanne chose the name Gloria, after her favorite doll. Within a few months, the resort season was on and the Steinems returned to Michigan.

Summers at Clark Lake were a tonic for Ruth, who still suffered from periods of anxiety and nameless fears. The economy had improved by the middle of the 1930s, and people again returned to the resort. There were lawn games and water sports, entertainment on the pier, camp fires and tall tales. Ruth and Leo worked hard to keep the resort running and Susanne was old enough to pitch in. There was always a pair of arms eager to cuddle the baby for an hour or two.

Life was almost idyllic during the summer of 1934, but with Labor Day came the close of the resort season and the start of Leo's travels on the road. Ruth felt more isolated than ever. Caring for the girls in the deserted resort stressed Ruth's fragile spirit.

As the Michigan winter settled in, with its storms and howling winds, Ruth's old fears began to haunt her. They had no car or phone to make contact with friends or family. Susanne was in school and Ruth was desperate for adult companionship, so desperate that one day she decided to walk the four or five miles to the nearest town in hope of finding someone, anyone, to talk with.

She bundled herself and Gloria in their warmest clothes and began walking, the family dog scampering along beside them. As they walked down a long hill a car came speeding over the crest, hit the dog, and sped away. Ruth ran to its side—it was still alive but critically injured. She cradled the dog in one arm, Gloria in the other, and waited on the side of the road, hoping another car would come along to help them. They waited there, Ruth, Gloria, and the dog, whimpering and crying in turns, until darkness descended and the little dog finally died.

That was, Ruth later told Gloria, her "breaking point." When Leo returned from his road trip she told him, "From now on, I'm going with you. I won't bother you. I'll just sit in the car. But I can't be alone again."

Chapter Two

A Child's Worst Fears

With Ruth and the girls traveling with him, Leo no longer had to restrict his territory. He bought a used travel trailer and hitched it to the back of the family sedan. This became the Steinem home as they spent winters crossing the southern half of the country, from California to Florida. Leo bought goods in small towns and tried to sell them at a profit in large cities. He was an entertainer as well as a dreamer, and during the long drives he entertained his family with jokes and stories.

There were few opportunities for Susanne, and later Gloria, to attend school for any length of time. But with her teaching certificate in hand, Ruth fended off the occasional truant officer while the girls educated themselves by reading everything they could get their hands on. Despite the mental illness that continued to plague her, Ruth had a remarkable ability to assure the girls that they were loved without reservation, and that she respected them as well. Leo, too, was able to give Susanne and Gloria a sense of security.

Gradually, though, Ruth's illness began to overwhelm

her. Since her hospitalization in 1930, Ruth was never without her prescription of what the family called "Doc Howard's Medicine." She needed it to sleep without hallucinating and hearing the voices that sometimes threatened her. But after she took a dose of the powerful drug, she seemed intoxicated. It became a vicious cycle: the more of the drug she took, the less she was able to handle life without it.

Surprisingly, Gloria's memories of her early child-hood were mostly positive. She read and reread books that became her beloved companions, working her way "through the entirety of Nancy Drew, Godey's Lady's Books, and the Theosophical Library."

"Louisa May Alcott was my friend," she later re-called. "I read all her adult novels as well as her young ones, and used to fantasize endlessly that she would come back to life and I could show her all the new things in the world."

Although Leo had the temperament of a gypsy and was sometimes financially irresponsible, he was al-ways optimistic and loving. Gloria said, "He treated me like a friend, asked my advice, enjoyed my company, and thus let me know that I was loved. Even in the hardest of times, of which there were many, I knew with a child's unerring sense of fairness that he was treating me as well as he treated himself."

Gloria had a great deal of freedom during the sum-mers at Clark Lake. Her childhood was ". . . a great time of running wild, catching turtles and minnows and set-ting them free again . . . wearing a bathing suit all day long and sleeping in a little office behind the dance hall to the sounds of [Big Band legends] Gene Krupa or Wayne King or the Andrews Sisters."

Ruth was going deeper into her own world and was becoming agoraphobic—afraid of crowds—and was sometimes unable to leave the house. One of Gloria's early memories "was of brushing her hair or dabbing powder on her pale cheeks while she sat docile as a child, depending on me to 'fix her up' for a rare outing."

At the resort, Gloria became comfortable talking with adults from all walks of life. She learned that her thoughts and beliefs—whether childish or mature, sensible or outrageous—were valued simply because they were hers. She began to cherish honesty and to feel true compassion. The Steinem family finances soon took another downturn when the U.S. entered World War II in December 1941. The carefree mood of the late 1930s was soon gone. Gas rationing made it difficult for people to make non-essential trips. The Steinems were forced to close the resort, and Gloria had to leave the home she loved best. In order to make a living, Leo would have to spend more time on the road buying and selling antiques. Because his traveling was necessary for him to support his family, Leo was granted gas tickets.

By 1944, Susanne was studying at prestigious Smith College in Northampton, Massachusetts. Ruth decided to move there with Gloria. At first it seemed to be an excellent change. Ruth's mental condition stabilized, and she was happy and functioning well as a mother.

Gloria spent her summers at her family's Michigan resort, Clark Lake. Here she is pictured on Easter Sunday, 1944, with a plate of eggs. *(Sophia Smith Collection, Smith College)*

But a year later she and Gloria moved back to Ohio, where Ruth had inherited the Nuneviller family home in East Toledo.

The once-proud working class neighborhood now suffered from neglect. The Nuneviller home's former days as a farmhouse were long gone. Many of the other homes had been torn down or made into cheap rooming houses, and a major highway passed close by the Nuneviller's front door. Ruth rented out the upper floors of the house, and she and Gloria made their home in a basement room behind the furnace.

With Leo gone most of the time and Susanne busy with school and preparing to enter the work world, Ruth and Gloria were left to fend for themselves. Ruth's mental condition deteriorated. She lived in a nightmare much of the time, rarely having a firm grasp on reality. She would ask Gloria whether German troops had reached their street yet, or if Susanne had been killed in an accident. If Gloria was late returning from school, Ruth would call the police to report her missing, often running through the neighborhood in her nightgown looking for her.

Now twelve years old, Gloria lived in a fantasy world of her own. She dreamed of her "real" parents showing up one day to reclaim her and take her to a better life. She haunted the public library, finding refuge in the pages of books. Gloria was able to build emotional walls that separated her from the sad reality of her home. Gloria could not depend on Ruth, neither emotionally nor maternally.

"I remember so well the dread of not knowing who I would find when I came home," Gloria recalled years later. "A mother whose speech was slurred by tranquilizers, a woman wandering in the neighborhood not sure of where she was, or a loving and sane woman who asked me about my school day. I created a cheerful front and took refuge in constant reading and after-school jobs—anything to divert myself (and others) from the realities of my life."

One of the benefits of their years living in the travel trailer was that Gloria became well-accustomed to cramped spaces. What they lacked in amenities, they made up for with creativity. Gloria remembers stacking old magazines in the shape of a chair, then covering it with an old throw.

But there were things that no amount of creativity could overcome. Rats sometimes invaded the house. Gloria was actually bitten one time, and somehow Ruth pulled herself together enough to get her to the hospital for treatment. Ruth despaired that this was the best she could provide for her own child. Her worries were compounded when she and Leo decided to end their marriage. As time passed, Leo saw his children less, and his financial contributions to the family were irregular.

Gloria grew to her full adult height of five-foot-seven at a young age. She took dancing lessons, which proved to be among the greatest joys of her life. Her teacher suggested that Gloria might enjoy dancing with a group of teens who performed regularly at the local Eagle's Club—the factory workers' equivalent of the

Elks or Masons—and other community organization. Although she was not legally of age, the twelve-year-old looked the part, and she desperately needed the ten dollars she could earn each night. She became comfortable in front of audiences (as long as she did not have to speak), and she gained poise and confidence.

Gloria did not invite friends to her home or leave much of an impression with teachers or schoolmates, but the atmosphere in East Toledo made a lifelong impression on her. One of the strongest memories was of how terribly girls were treated if they became pregnant. "Shotgun" weddings forced many teens into marriage and parenthood. Pregnant girls were automatically expelled from school and rarely allowed back in after childbirth. Their mundane lives from that time on offered few opportunities for education or meaningful work.

"Women were so clearly divided into victims and nice girls," Gloria explained. "And if you became a victim, not a nice girl, your life was over." She vowed that she would never allow herself to become trapped. Instead of dreaming of being rescued by a handsome hero, Gloria dreamed of rescuing others.

Between school, after-school activities, and her jobs dancing and, later, as a salesgirl, Gloria took care of her mother. Despite all their problems, Gloria and Ruth maintained their love and respect for each other. Gloria recognized that although Ruth could not take care of her, "I always knew my mother loved me . . ."

As Gloria continued to grow up, the bright days in

their lives became fewer and farther between. What little money they had was nearly gone by 1951. The old Nuneviller house had decayed to the point that the city condemned it. Although the church next door bought the property, Ruth and Gloria faced homelessness because Ruth was determined to save the proceeds from the sale for Gloria's college education. Ruth wanted Gloria to attend Smith College, as Susanne had.

Leo took time from his travels, and Susanne, who was then working in Washington, D.C., made an emergency trip to Toledo. Susanne wanted to take Gloria back with her to Washington, to live with her and finish high school. She insisted that Leo take responsibility for Ruth. Gloria's hopes skyrocketed—she imagined that living with Susanne was a chance for a normal life—and then tumbled into despair when Leo refused. Only when Leo saw how upset Gloria was did he relent. "All right," Gloria remembers him saying. "But one year is all. We're synchronizing our watches."

Chapter Three

Independence

During the seven years Gloria spent living with her mentally ill mother, she had held out hope that Ruth would be cured. Susanne, though, believed that the Ruth she had known as a child was gone forever, and that it was time to find a permanent place for her care. As Gloria finished her last year of high school in the Georgetown section of Washington, D.C., Susanne began to look for an institution in which to place Ruth.

Because of the great number of World War II soldiers who returned with combat-related psychological illnesses, attitudes toward the mentally ill in America had begun to improve. Until then, most institutions were little more than warehouses, and mental illness was viewed as a personal failure, a weakness of character that the patient could overcome if an appropriate effort was made. Susanne was able to find a psychiatric hospital in Baltimore where patients received the kind of mental therapy that could allow them to eventually function in their communities. Although it was not easy to convince Ruth—or Leo and Gloria—that she should enter the institute, Susanne finally convinced her family that long-term treatment was for the best.

In the fall of 1952, Gloria entered Smith College free from worries about her mother. Smith, located in Northampton, Massachusetts, was a beautiful campus. One of the so-called "Seven Sisters" of female colleges, Smith's students were mostly from more affluent backgrounds than Gloria was. Despite this, Gloria loved everything about Smith—the classes, the faculty, her fellow students. She never talked to her classmates about Ruth's illness. Instead, she became known for her humor and her stories about her carefree summers at Clark Lake and on the road in the travel trailer. "We've just finished washing last year's dishes," she would jokingly say.

To Gloria, the difference between herself and the typical Smith students, who usually came from privileged families, was meaningless. "I had so little experience with the agonies of social difference . . . that I simply didn't worry about it." While most students wore cashmere sweaters and designer clothes, Gloria was happy in her jeans and sweatshirts (this was long before they became fashionable). She would teach classmates how to iron and how to put on makeup; in exchange they would tutor her in French or math. She remembers that kind of bartering as an important lesson: "Don't worry about your background," she says, "whether it's odd or ordinary, use it, build on it." Gloria was also appreciated for her listening skills. "When you spoke to her," one classmate recalled, "she looked at you."

Gloria spent her summers in Washington with Ruth and Susanne. She worked at a municipal swimming pool in one of the city's black communities. Although she was the only white person there, her coworkers helped her to feel accepted. She identified with the people at the pool and thus—after a few of the typical skirmishes to test the new kid on the block—she was accepted as just one of the lifeguards.

Gloria spent her junior year studying in Geneva, Switzerland. She was fascinated with the new places, new people, and new language. The following summer, she studied at Oxford, England. On her return to Smith that fall for her senior year, she spoke with one of the vocational counselors about going to law school. "Why study three extra years and end up in the back room of some law firm doing research and typing," the counselor asked, "when you can graduate from Smith and do research and typing right away?" Even in a prestigious college such as Smith, women were not expected to have a life-long career. Gloria later remembered a Smith commencement speech given by Alistair Cooke in 1954:

> At this moment, ridiculous though it may seem, the fortune of you here is being decided by anonymous young men who are packing their bags in New Haven, Connecticut, in Cambridge, Massachusetts, in Princeton, New Jersey . . . It may not be the proper thing for a commencement speaker to begin this way by wishing you a happy marriage. But . . . since it is the supreme role which all of you will sooner or later hanker after . . . it seems to me realistic to start by

recognizing, on this spring morning, the main direction in which your fancies turn.

This was *not* the message Gloria wanted to hear. She wanted nothing to do with more full-time care taking, whether it was for her mother, or for a husband and children. There was so much she wanted to do, so many places to travel, people to meet, cultures to learn about. She could think of nothing she wanted more than to be on her own, free and independent.

Despite this attitude, Gloria got engaged during her senior year. She loved her fiancé and part of her wanted to follow the traditional path into marriage and family, although another side of her wanted to be responsible only to herself. She was torn in two directions and struggled with her future. Finally, when she was offered a one-year post-graduate fellowship to study in India, she broke her engagement.

Before she could enter India, Gloria had to go to England to await her visa. There she discovered that she was pregnant. She knew that her decision—whether to have the baby and raise it alone, give it up for adoption, or to have an abortion (which was then legal in England, though not in the U.S.)—would profoundly affect the rest of her life.

She remembered the girls she had known in Toledo who had been forced into marriage and motherhood before they were ready; she knew about the stigma placed on unwed mothers. She decided to have an abortion. Under British law at the time, two doctors had to sign an authorization before it could be done. One of the doctors told Gloria he would sign under two conditions: first, that she not tell anyone he had signed for her; second, that "she promise to do what she really wanted with her life."

In India, one of her fellowship responsibilities was to write about what she saw and did while she was there. These travelogues about "the mysterious East," she thought, would serve as a writer's resume that would help her to become a successful writer.

When Gloria arrived in India she found it not mysterious in the least. Instead she was a little overwhelmed by the poverty and the crowded cities. The Indians lived in a strict society in which citizens belonged to certain castes, or social classes. Gloria, however, did not let the rigid Indian caste system hinder her, and she began to identify with the poor.

She soon found that Western dress hindered her from blending in, so she darkened her hair and wore a sari, the traditional Indian dress. She got a job writing a promotional booklet, "The Thousand Indias," for the Indian Tourist Bureau and made extra money by making sandals. Of her travels, even during the caste riots in southern India, Gloria wrote, "I discovered that a Westerner in a sari was no more strange than someone from a distant part of India might have been, and that my English-with-a-little Hindi was as useful . . . as some of the other fourteen major languages of India."

Gloria was told that if she wanted to see the *real* India she should travel to the state of Madras in the southeast. Forgoing the privileges assumed by most Westerners, Gloria packed into a third class train to travel through the country with impoverished Indians.

Arriving in Madras, Gloria met up with a small group of Gandhians, followers of the philosophy of Mahatma Gandhi. Gandhi, who led a thirty-year nonviolent campaign against the British occupation of India, had been assassinated less than ten years earlier, in 1948. But his followers continued his work for all castes "to be respected as one, all religions as one."

At the time of her visit, caste riots had broken out in rural areas, villages had been burned and people were killed. The caste conflicts were fueled by local politicians who sought conflict for their own gain. The government had sealed the area off to keep the riots from spreading. The Gandhians were walking from village to village, holding meetings and urging villagers to respond with nonviolence rather than vengeance. "Instead of weapons," Gloria said of the Gandhians, "they were carrying only a cup and a comb, knowing that if the villagers wanted peace, they would feed and house the peacemakers, thus becoming part of the process."

The Gandhians asked Gloria to join them. They assured her that she would be accepted by the villagers. They needed her help because they, as men, would not be able to enter women's quarters to invite them to meetings. Gloria was intrigued, not only to work with Gandhian activists but to work with activists who encouraged women to join them. She stowed her extra clothing and personal items and traveled with only her sari, a towel, a cup and a comb. Gloria recalls this time:

> [W]e walked from one village to the next, sitting under trees for meetings in the cool of the early morning, walking during the heat of the day, and holding more meetings around kerosene lamps at night. Mostly, we just listened. There were so many stories of atrocities and vengeance . . . that it was hard to imagine how it could end. But gradually, people expressed relief at having been listened to, at seeing neighbors who had been afraid to come out of their houses, and at hearing facts brought by [the Gandhian] team, for the rumors were even more terrible than the events themselves. To my amazement . . . meetings often ended with village leaders pledging to take no revenge on caste groups whose members had attacked their group in a neighboring village, and to continue meetings of their own.

The Gandhian's organizing guidelines made a profound impact on Gloria as she helped implement them in the villages:

> *If you do something the people care about, the people will take care of you. If you want people to listen to you, you have to listen to them. If you hope people will change how they live, you have to know how they live. If you want people to see you, you have to sit down with them eye-to-eye.*

"Most of us have a few events that divide our lives into 'before' and 'after,' " says Gloria. "This was one for me."

Chapter Four

Writer and Activist

Soon after Gloria returned to the U.S. in 1958, another young American—Martin Luther King, Jr.—was preparing to leave for India. While studying divinity at Boston University, King had become intrigued with Gandhi. He thought Gandhi's nonviolent strategy and tactics could be adapted to the fledgling American civil rights movement. King was laying the groundwork for one of the most important social revolutions in U.S. history, the fight against legal racial segregation in the United States.

In the years immediately after the end of World War II, most Americans concentrated on returning to normalcy. After the years of upheaval caused by the Great Depression and the war, most citizens seemed to be content to focus on finishing their education, finding a job, starting a family, and purchasing the vast array of consumer items being turned out by American factories.

But during the mid-1950s, a gradual but unrelenting movement toward changing the societal status quo began to develop. African Americans, especially in the South, began to speak out and protest against the Jim Crow laws that remanded them to second class citizenship. Beginning with the 1956 Montgomery Bus Boycott, led by Martin Luther King, Jr., the nation was soon witness to a massive move toward social change, unlike any since the Civil War.

By the early 1960s, other protest movements began to organize. As the war in Vietnam developed so did a movement to end the United States participation in that war. Folk singers such as Bob Dylan and Joan Baez became famous singing about the evils of war, greed, and racism. After President John Kennedy was assassinated in 1963, it seemed that many of the protest movements left the college campuses and coffee houses and burst into the headlines.

A move toward women's rights, however, was slow to develop. Although many of the front line workers in the Civil Rights movement were women, they received little of the attention or acclaim. The same could be said of the anti-war movement, where names such as Abbie Hoffman and Tom Hayden became famous, but the women who did much of the organizing were little-known. Even the decades of women leaders, reaching back to the nineteenth century, were almost unknown to most Americans. Women were too often left out of the history books.

As Gloria wrote later, "[T]he educational shame was this: no one *did* tell us." Ignored in textbooks, she said, "were the nineteenth century works of black and white feminists, from Elizabeth Cady Stanton to Frederick Douglass, who had explained this race-sex parallel at learned and courageous length in the suffragist and abolitionist movements. I was told only that women were 'given' the right to vote, a one-sentence distortion of a century of struggle that did nothing to shake my assumption that power was located somewhere other than within myself." It would be almost a decade before the demand for equal treatment of women became a prominent, "front burner" issue.

On Gloria's return to Washington, she was much relieved to find that Ruth had improved during her hospitalization. Susanne had married, and the newly-weds opened their home to Ruth for visits that gradually became longer and longer. Ruth's old terrors could still overwhelm her, and she would return for a short stay at the Baltimore hospital or a nearby Quaker half-way house, where she felt comfortable and safe. Her relapses would continue to recur for years.

Gloria, meanwhile, was trying to find a job. Knowing that Ruth was in capable hands, she headed to New York City to pursue her dream of becoming a professional writer. She found that women writers were rarely hired for "serious" reporting, and most of New York's publishing industry kept women in secretarial work. For that, Gloria was told, she was "overqualified."

Late in 1959, Gloria finally received a job offer. It was not a writing job and it was not in New York, but it fit perfectly with her awakening awareness of social causes. She moved to Cambridge, Massachusetts, to become the director of an organization called Independent Research Service, one of many student-oriented organizations secretly funded by the Central Intelligence Agency.

Like many Americans, Gloria was unaware of the CIA's secret activities during the years after World War II. The full scope of the agency's role in creating international turmoil, including political coups and assassinations, would not be uncovered for decades.

The CIA recognized the power of student-led movements. Through funding the Independent Research Service, the CIA sent young Americans to participate in Communist Youth Conferences (until that year held only in communist countries) where they could meet their Soviet-sponsored peers from Third World countries. Despite the programs's stated goal to demonstrate the free and open exchange of ideas that were constitutionally guaranteed in the U.S., many Americans believed the CIA had an ulterior motive to recruit an international cadre of student spies. At the time, for Gloria and most Americans, the news that a major federal agency was backing the Independent Research Service was strictly positive. She "remembers feeling relief that someone understood the importance of the noncommunist left in general, and students in particular."

Though naive about the CIA, Gloria was far from ignorant of the world of international politics. She wrote her aunt about her experiences from a festival in Vienna: "I think it struck a lot of us the same way. It's a realization that, pretty often, the men who run Everything [sic] are just guys with gravy on their vests and not too much between the ears and that you (one) can do something toward putting monkey wrenches in the totalitarian works and convincing the uncommitted that it's smarter to stay that way than to trade Western colonialism for Communist imperialism."

If the CIA's motive was to use Gloria to recruit spies, it failed. But neither was she a dupe of the communists. She simply got busy doing the best job possible of helping to organize the festival. "When we arrived," said Gloria, "and we discovered how shorthanded the Austrians and others were in their efforts to counteract the festival, we hatched plans with them and ended up by opening three Vienna offices instead of one and doing press and coordinating-type things for all the non-communist groups instead of just the Americans."

After finishing her work on the festival and closing the office, Gloria was eager to give New York City another try. This time, though, she was determined to make it on her own as a freelance writer. She had taken care of herself most of her life, and she had lived in India with only a cup, a comb, and a sari. She felt that she could survive *anywhere*.

Although Gloria had more impressive writing credentials than most males her age, she had trouble finding writing assignments. Women writers were still confined to the Three Fs: fashion, food, and family. Gloria wanted to write about issues and ideas, she wanted to challenge and be challenged, but most editors she met would not give her a chance.

There was, however, one other writing venue that was occasionally open to women: celebrity profiles. There were a few New York magazines that refused to publish fluff celebrity pieces, preferring instead a more honest look at celebrity subjects. *Show* was one of them, *Esquire* was another. Gloria began getting assignments from both. Soon the editors of *Show* and *Esquire* realized that Gloria was an excellent writer, and that she was disciplined. She produced top quality, intelligent work on time, on subject, and on the assigned word count. Editors loved her.

She was not intimidated by wealth or fame, and even the most cantankerous celebrities would open up to Gloria's warmth and genuine interest. Many of her profiles were of famous writers of the era, including James Baldwin, Dorothy Parker, and Truman Capote. Gloria was enthralled. Not only was she able to write substantial articles about interesting and gifted artists, she was learning more of her craft from them as well.

Freelancing, as sporadic and insecure as it was, gave Gloria the freedom she craved, along with the self-discipline needed to meet deadlines. Writing never came quickly or easily for Gloria, but it was always rewarding. "For me," she wrote, "writing is the only thing that passes the three tests of metier: (1) when I'm doing it, I don't feel that I should be doing something else instead; (2) it produces a sense of accomplishment and, once in a while, pride; and (3) it's frightening."

Through her profiles, Gloria got to know a host of New York's movers and shakers, including society people and politicians, as well as celebrities. Among her most important contacts in those early years was *Esquire* editor Clay Felker, who gave Gloria her first serious writing assignment for the magazine. He later sought Gloria's help in founding *New York* magazine in 1968.

By 1961, Gloria's freelance assignments were taking her beyond New York City. During one of these trips she received a call telling her that her father Leo had been hospitalized following a car accident in California. She was on her way to his side, waiting to change planes in Chicago on April 21, when she was paged for an emergency call from Susanne. Leo Steinem had died in the hospital of internal bleeding.

Back in New York, other changes were taking place as well. The $150 a month rent on her tiny apartment was about to be increased. Gloria found a roommate, artist Barbara Nessim, and they moved into a studio apartment. It would have been unbearably cramped for most people, but Gloria was used to living in small spaces with few possessions, as was Barbara. Theirs was a comfortable match for two independent women.

Financially, both women were struggling. Although Gloria was writing for top magazines and was praised for her talent, most major articles were nevertheless reserved for male writers who were paid more than the few women journalists. Her first major assignment came from *Esquire* in 1963—an article discussing the effects of the new birth control pill on college women. Barbara, who was also a freelancer, met many of the same kinds of obstacles as Gloria.

Gloria also found an outlet for her irrepressible sense of humor in 1960, when she began writing for a new satire magazine, *Help! For Tired Minds*, a one-person operation of Harvey Kurtzman, the creator of *Mad* magazine. Kurtzman remembers Gloria for much more than her writing talent. He said she had "chutzpah," recruiting comedians such as Sid Caesar, Dick Van Dyke, and Jackie Gleason for the magazine.

Gloria's level of comfort around diverse people, nurtured during those summers at Clark Lake and her time in India, was an invaluable asset in her career. Gloria used these assets both in her private and professional life. College students, white and black, were in the forefront of the civil rights movement; a movement against U.S. involvement in Southeast Asia was developing; and there was a fledgling movement among migrant farm workers on the West Coast. In New York, Gloria began volunteering to help organize and fund protest activities. She immediately felt at home with the activists—she had discovered in India that organizing was in her blood.

This interest in social movements, however, ran up against the same barrier: her gender. She wanted to write about these movements, but she was barred because women were locked out of writing on serious, controversial issues. There was also a general editorial policy, which applied to both men and women, that writers would have a conflict of interest writing about issues they were involved in.

Gloria set out on another path. She became, on her

own time, an organizer and fundraiser for the causes she held dear. She began calling on her celebrity contacts, asking them to donate their time, their names, their money, or all three. She brought together activists and artists, students and politicians, radicals and philanthropists.

Gloria soon found herself amongst New York's liberal "in" crowd, who had been labeled "radical chic" by conservative journalist Tom Wolfe. Occasionally, she even appeared in photos on the society pages and, although she was still struggling financially, Gloria managed to dress the part with clothes borrowed or bought wholesale. Like Leo, she had a fascination with show biz, and whether at small discotheques or big benefits with live music, she could dance to her heart's content.

Chapter Five

Awakening

The spark that ignited the modern feminist movement was a book, *The Feminine Mystique*, written by Betty Friedan, and published in 1963. However, the group that the book focused on, middle-class homemakers, did not respond as a mass, and most ignored it altogether. A small minority took heart at Friedan's exposure of the sexism that ruled their lives and began to talk. Some even began to organize. Other women, while recognizing the restrictions that sexism imposed on their lives, felt that civil rights and the Vietnam War were more critical concerns and that feminism should take a back seat.

Gloria felt she simply could not identify with Friedan's typical frustrated homemaker. She had gone to college, traveled to Europe and India, and was already in the workforce. "I shared the reaction of many working-class women and women of color," she remembered later, reflecting on the reaction to Friedan's book. "I support women who want to get out of the suburbs and into jobs . . . but I'm already in the workforce and getting screwed. The women's movement isn't for me."

At the time, Gloria's personal inspiration was Holly Golightly, the protagonist in Truman Capote's short novel *Breakfast at Tiffany's*. Gloria "identified with the poor and prematurely responsible childhood [Holly] had escaped by walking down a dirt road a little farther every day—until finally she just kept on going."

In essence, Gloria *became* Holly Golightly, who was later immortalized by Audrey Hepburn in the movie version: She streaked her hair, wore kerchiefs and over-sized sunglasses, short skirts ("satisfyingly unlady-like"), and otherwise "patched myself together with just the right combination of flaunting and hiding."

Flaunting was a skill that Gloria had to adopt for an undercover assignment for the magazine *Show*. Hugh Hefner, the publisher of *Playboy* magazine, was about to open a Playboy Club in New York. Ads appeared everywhere, it seemed, recruiting young, beautiful women to work as Playboy Bunnies in the club. They were promised glamour, excitement, and incredible pay.

At the time, *Playboy* magazine was a publishing phenomenon—literate, political, and funny, it was also a "girlie" magazine, featuring bare breasts and bottoms of beautiful women. These women were called "Bunnies," and Hefner's genius was in making his readers believe that because they read *Playboy,* they were just the kind of sophisticated, suave men that Bunnies would swoon over. Then he began opening the doors of Playboy Clubs to give those readers a chance to enhance their fantasies in the presence of scantily-clad waitresses dressed as "Playboy Bunnies."

Show wanted to capitalize on the curiosity surrounding the new Clubs, and after much discussion, Gloria was chosen to go undercover as a Playboy Bunny. Tall, willowy, and gregarious, she appeared to fit the Bunny mold. *Show* editors thought that she would be able to land a job easily.

Only it was not so easy. First, Gloria would have to lie—about her age (she was twenty-eight; the maximum age for Bunnies was twenty-four), about her background and job experience (a Smith-educated professional writer would raise suspicions), and even her name (she became Marie Catherine Ochs, after her grandmother—"it sounds too square to be phony," Gloria quipped.) The Bunny application process was the most nerve-racking she had ever experienced.

But that was just the beginning. Wearing the infamous Bunny costume for a full eight-hour shift was torture. "The whole costume was darted and seamed until it was two inches smaller than any of my measurements everywhere except the bust," Gloria wrote. The extra space in the bust was called "the vault," for not only was the space padded with plastic dry cleaner bags to give the illusion of oversized breasts, it was also where the Bunnies kept their tips.

Bunnies were required to pay $2.50 a day for upkeep and cleaning of their costumes, to buy their own black tights, makeup and three-quarter inch eyelashes, and dyed-to-match, pointy-toed, three-inch (minimum) high heels. After just four hours on her feet her first night, Gloria felt as if she were in a body cast that was two

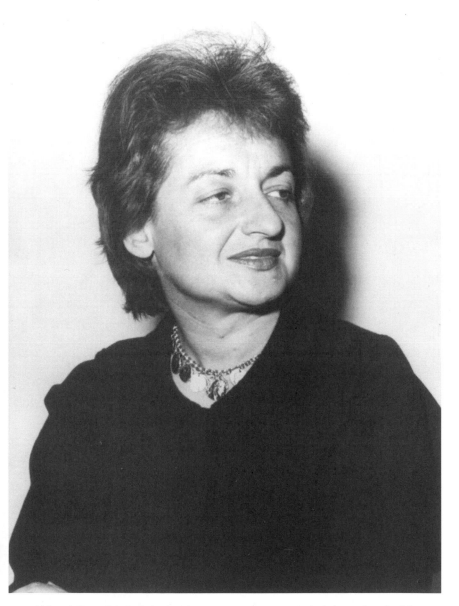

Although Betty Friedan's book, *The Feminine Mystique*, sparked the modern feminist movement in America, Gloria Steinem did not feel the book addressed the issues she faced as a young, female journalist. *(Library of Congress)*

sizes too small. The Bunny costume cut off circulation and constricted her waist and ribs so it was impossible to take a full breath. Once, she was in the break room trying to find a way to lean in her costume so she could massage her swollen feet when a maintenance man suggested she put a cold bottle of soda on the floor and roll her arches over it. As she did so, he told her that even though he took out garbage for a living, he would rather have his job than hers.

It did not take Gloria long to discover that the promises of glamour and riches rarely if ever matched the reality of Bunny life. Trainees were told they would start at New York City's minimum wage ($50 for a forty-hour week), that they could keep only cash tips (but would be fired if they told a customer cash was preferred), and that tips charged to credit cards would be split with the club. When Gloria mentioned the disparity between the advertised and actual pay to another Bunny, the woman responded, "Two hundred dollars to three hundred a *what*? I got a hundred and eight dollars this week, and the girl with the biggest check got a hundred and forty-five."

A week of unpaid training, followed by a week of paid agony were as much as Gloria could take. Of her last day on the job, she wrote, "Somehow, the usual tail pullings and propositions and pinching and ogling seemed all the more depressing when, outside this windowless room of perpetual night, the sun was shining."

Meanwhile, Gloria's earlier *Esquire* article on the contraceptive revolution had created a stir and accelerated her freelancing career. Editors recognized her talent and a few offered a choice assignment or two on an increased pay scale, though still not equal to a man's. Then the appearance of the Playboy exposé, under the title "A Bunny's Tale: *Show's* 'First Exposé for Intelligent People,' " changed her life almost overnight.

Gloria believed she had written a profoundly anti-Bunny article. So did Hugh Hefner, who sued Gloria and a newspaper in which she was quoted for a million dollars. (He did not win.) But what disturbed her were the letters she received from women of other Playboy Clubs who were threatened for trying to unionize to get better working conditions. Even more disturbing were letters from women wanting to know how *they* could become Bunnies. She always discouraged them: "It was still one of the two or three most depressing experiences in my life," she wrote to one.

Although she was now a near celebrity herself, the old dichotomy still existed. She was living with her roommate in their tiny apartment, with no space to completely unpack her clothes and papers, while at the same time she was being invited to swishy parties and nightclubs and dating men who were on the fast track to power or fame or both. Much later, Gloria would remember this time as one of trying to fit in, but not quite making it. She would fantasize, "trying on the name and life of each man I thought I might marry—thought I would *have* to marry eventually if I was to be a whole person . . .

"*I'll definitely get married*, I kept thinking, but not

right now. *There's this one thing I want to do first . . ."*

Gloria later wrote that she could not have traded her independent life for security and a more comfortable home because "that was the way I had protected myself against getting attached to places as a vagabond child."

Gloria fit in well with her writer and artist friends—she was beautiful, stylish, articulate, gracious, and funny—and she delighted in being able to talk about the major issues of the day. She was an independent woman who did not try to hide her intellect, who was keenly aware of weighty issues and was not afraid to discuss them. She treated everyone—men, women, cab drivers, celebrities—as equals.

As relaxed as she made those around her feel, Gloria never quite got past feeling like an outsider at large social gatherings. She was still a jeans-and-sweatshirt person at heart, more at home with ghetto kids at the Washington pool than at formal gatherings in New York. One-on-one, she made deep and lasting friendships, but the social scene itself—especially when a relationship with one of the men of these circles became serious—was uncharted and uncomfortable territory.

During the time she was dating director Mike Nichols, for example, she would sit beside him at a dinner party and notice that her identity was being absorbed into his. Mike and his work were just becoming important on Broadway, Gloria and her work were merely interesting sidelights. And of course she would give up her identity if they married; she would become an appendage—*Mrs.* Mike Nichols, not Gloria Steinem.

Chapter Six

The Road to Feminism

As the 1960s developed, Gloria's activism on behalf of civil rights and anti-war movements took time away from her writing. It seemed to her to be the first time American politics were inclusive and open to everyone.

In 1967, anti-Vietnam War activists began to rally around senator Eugene McCarthy, who was running for the 1968 Democratic Party nomination. Gloria did volunteer work for the McCarthy campaign. But as the 1968 campaign year approached, Gloria developed serious reservations about McCarthy. The Senator, who had a patrician method of speaking and writing, seemed unable to connect with the poor and racial minorities. Around this time she met another Senator, George McGovern, who impressed her as a strong, kind man who was as concerned as she was about a whole range of issues, while McCarthy was focused on ending the war in Vietnam. Soon she had shifted her support from McCarthy to McGovern and became a publicity manager for his campaign. She wrote issue pamphlets and fund-raising letters. She also set up interviews and meet-

ings with McGovern and editorial boards at major newspapers and national magazines.

McGovern encouraged Gloria to accompany him to
these meetings. She was an experienced journalist, and
he knew that her insight and experience could be invaluable. The male editorial boards took a different
perspective. She soon realized that her presence stifled
the editors in small, but meaningful, ways. The men
stumbled to avoid swear words, and even the traditional
passing out of cigars was eliminated. "Apparently,"
Gloria wrote, ". . . the appearance of women at these
events is not part of the ritual."

Although McGovern did not win the Democratic
nomination in 1968, the experience was invaluable for
Gloria. She was able to see how the editorial boards
operated at the nation's most prestigious newspapers
and magazines. She also became more aware of the
growing feminist movement and began to change her
opinion that the movement was mainly for housewives.

In 1966, Betty Friedan and other middle-class feminists had organized the National Organization for
Women (NOW), and the group had grown rapidly.
Gloria's writing assignments began to include articles
about the women's movement, and soon she found that,
"Feminist ideas began to explode . . . and helped us all
to realize that we shared an overarching problem: being
judged on how we looked instead of what was in our
heads and hearts." Small things such as "feeling we
couldn't go to the grocery store without lipstick, or
giving more thought to what we wore than what we

read. I abandoned clothes anxiety with relief and evolved a simple, comfortable, jeans-sweater-and-boots uniform that I wore for one entire decade."

Nineteen sixty-eight was an astonishing year in American history: Martin Luther King, Jr. and Robert Kennedy were assassinated; police and anti-war protesters fought at the Democratic Convention in Chicago; student protests begun at Columbia University and the University of California at Berkeley spread to schools and colleges across the country. California farm workers, under the leadership of another Gandhi-inspired activist, César Chávez, were organizing and striking for decent salary and working conditions.

During these hectic years Gloria continued to write. She also became involved in the founding of a new publication with her friend and first editor, Clay Felker, whom she had known since her early days in New York. When Clay decided to launch his own magazine, called *New York*, the first person he thought of was Gloria. He had been impressed from the beginning with her talent and her political insight. She became *New York*'s contributing editor as well as its political columnist. "For the first time, I wasn't writing about one thing, while caring about something else," she said.

Gloria went to Harlem to do interviews following the King assassination; she went to California to report on the farm workers movement. But she did not *just* report. Her research on the farm workers and their commitment to Gandhian nonviolence drew her into an activist role with the group. Gloria, however, was uncomfortable with the majority of the farm workers' sexual bias, which took for granted men's right to control women and their bodies, but she could not ignore their plight. Most farm workers had large families to support, were uneducated, impoverished, and constantly on the move following the harvest.

By this time, Gloria had moved into a brownstone apartment of her own, though most of her possessions were still in suitcases and boxes. She got a message one day to call a farm workers organizer named Marion Moses, who had arrived in New York several weeks earlier to raise support for the group. Marion was discouraged and getting desperate. She had spent weeks knocking on doors, following leads, and trying to live on the five dollars a week the farm workers could afford to pay her. Marion remembered her first phone conversation with Gloria: "I called, she called back. I can still hear that wonderful voice."

Gloria opened her apartment to Marion; she lent her clothes and introduced her to her friends in entertainment, the arts, and philanthropy. Together they got interviews for Chávez with *Time*, *Life*, and *Look*, an appearance on the *Today* show, and a follow-up cover story in *Time*.

They organized a benefit for the farm workers at Carnegie Hall that brought hundreds of supporters, including a small core of celebrities. Thirty-thousand dollars was taken in at the door, with later donations from Jackie Kennedy, Woody Allen, and other notables. The media attention and money helped propel the group

Gloria worked with United Farm Workers (UFW) organizer Marion Moses (left) to demand better working conditions and pay for migrant laborers in the United States and Mexico. Despite the UFW's concern for quality of life issues, the women found that many female farm workers suffered from sexism and abuse. *(Jane O'Reilly, photographer)*

and its charismatic leader into the national spotlight. Most importantly, the exposure lessened the violence and harassment the farm workers suffered when they tried to organize.

Despite the work of Gloria and Marion, who also served as a nurse and head of the farm workers' clinic, as well as the efforts put forth by volunteers from a predominantly female hospital workers union, they were largely ignored by the male leadership of the union. Even these victims of bigotry were blind to how they discounted women. Discrimination, Gloria realized, was such a massive problem—whether against blacks, Jews, farm workers, or women—that trying to tackle any isolated aspect of it would end in frustration.

Chapter Seven

Breakthrough

By 1969, Gloria had arrived at a personal and professional crossroads. The more aware she became of feminist issues, the more she understood that male professionals had a stake in keeping women out of *their* job market. Yet she had devoted most of her adult life to carving out a place for herself in the publishing world, a place where she had earned the respect of her colleagues and now had the influence to help other women strengthen their careers. The events of 1969 removed any remaining doubts Gloria had about feminism and propelled her into an international revolution. Until this point, she had, as she said, "learned to Uncle Tom with subtlety, logic, and humor. Sometimes I even believed it myself." She told herself, for example:

> My work won't interfere with marriage. After all, I
> can always keep my typewriter at home.
> I don't want to write about women's stuff. I want to
> write about foreign policy.
> He says I write like a man.

Gloria realized that she could suffer if she became an outspoken feminist. "(T)here seems to be no punishment inside the white male club that quite equals the ridicule and personal viciousness reserved for women who rebel . . . Any woman who chooses to behave like a full human being should be warned that the armies of the status quo will treat her as something of a dirty joke. That's their natural and first weapon."

One experience helped Gloria become more determined to fight for women's equality. Gloria had been assigned to interview a leading actor, and they arranged to meet for tea in the Palm Court of the glamorous Plaza Hotel, where he was staying. She arrived at the Plaza on time and waited in the lobby for the actor to join her. Her wait grew longer and longer, and she began to notice that a hotel official was watching her. The manager finally approached her and announced loudly that "unescorted ladies [were] absolutely not allowed" to stand in the lobby.

When Gloria tried to explain that she was a reporter assigned to interview a hotel guest, the manager took her by the arm and led her into the street. "I was humiliated: Did I look like a prostitute? Was my trench coat too battered—or not battered enough?"

Several weeks later, Gloria got another assignment to interview a guest at the Plaza. This time, she arranged to meet the celebrity in his suite in order to avoid another humiliation in the lobby. When she entered, though, she noticed the same manager and decided to stop for a moment to see what would happen.

Sure enough, the manager approached me with his same officious speech. But this time I was amazed to hear myself saying some very different things. I told him this was a public place where I had every legal right to be, and asked why he hadn't banished the several 'unescorted men' in the lobby who might be male prostitutes. I also pointed out that since hotel staffs were well known to supply call girls in return for a percentage of their pay, perhaps he was just worried about losing a commission.

He looked quite startled—and let me stay. I called my subject and suggested we have tea downstairs after all.

What had changed? "When I faced the hotel manager again," said Gloria, "I had glimpsed the world *as if women mattered*. By seeing through their eyes, I had begun to see through my own."

While Gloria's transformation was coming full circle, the society around her was as deeply entrenched as ever. For example, she received a call from George McGovern, who was preparing to run for president in 1972. She had been looking forward to a gathering of McGovern allies to plan his campaign, but the Senator called to inform her she could not come to the meeting. He explained that her invitation had been scrapped by one of his key strategists, who told McGovern emphatically, "no broads." Despite McGovern's defense of Gloria as one of his most valuable and skilled campaign workers, the strategist insisted, *no broads*.

Gloria knew that she had "raised as much money and

done as much political work as anyone in McGovern's last brief presidential effort," and she knew that McGovern had made a sincere effort to change the strategist's mind. She wondered what would have happened if the Senator had said *no blacks* or *no Jews,* but in the end she did not think it was worth a fight.

"I think it's precisely *because* the meeting was such a common incident," Gloria said at the time, and "*because* McGovern is the best of the political lot, that I feel so estranged.

"I realize that unless women organize, support each other, and force change, nothing basic is going to happen. Not even with the best of men. And I wonder: *Are women—including me—willing to face that?*"

One of those "best of men" was César Chávez, and once again Gloria found that despite their crucial work on behalf of the farm workers, most women were either invisible or relegated to lesser importance. Gloria had been a full-time volunteer recruiting political leaders and organizing media coverage for a massive 300-mile march from Delano, California, to Calexico, Mexico, where American and Mexican farm workers would meet at the border to "have a celebration and agree never to work against each other."

Gloria traveled with the marchers through the desert's 100-plus degree heat. She covered the march as a reporter, as well, and put all her expenses on her personal American Express card. She slept on garage or barn floors with the marchers until they reached Calexico.

She was still close to Marion Moses, the farm worker

Although Steinem was a long-time and valued campaigner for George McGovern, he would not allow women to help plan his 1972 presidential campaign. *(Library of Congress)*

nurse and organizer she had shared her apartment with, and together they began to realize that not only were women doing most of the work while the men received the credit, but many of the women's personal issues were being controlled by men. Marion began to see how a lack of birth control was causing serious health problems for the women she worked with. She was a Catholic and had always stood with the Church against abortion and contraception, but it tore her apart to see how many of these women were pregnant year after year, having children they could not afford to feed, and growing old before their time.

Marion could not stand silently by, doing nothing to prevent pregnancy-related medical problems—malnutrition, disease, and infant and maternal mortality. She felt that giving out information about birth control was a small compromise of her religious values.

Then, a mother of seven children, a diabetic with high blood pressure, came to her begging for birth control pills. Marion made another compromise and found a doctor who would prescribe the contraceptives. When he discovered that his wife was using contraception, the woman's husband became outraged. Chávez was outraged too when he learned of this, and he told Marion that she was never to advocate birth control to the women farm workers again.

Marion refused. "To deny the woman birth control was not medicine but dogma," wrote one observer. "She told Chavez that either she used her judgment or she quit. She stayed."

As it turned out, birth control, or more specifically women's right to control their bodies, was the pivotal issue in Gloria's feminist transformation.

Early in 1969, a group calling itself Redstockings made its first public appearance at a New York state legislative hearing on abortion law reform. The only people who had spoken before the legislators were fourteen men, doctors and psychiatrists, and one female, a nun. When members of Redstockings tried to take the microphone to tell their personal stories of abortion the meeting was abruptly adjourned. The group then organized a press conference where a dozen women were to talk about their own illegal abortions. Gloria went to cover the event for her column in *New York*.

Unsure of what to expect, Gloria entered the church basement to find an audience of some 300 women and men in rapt attention to the speakers. What she heard changed her life. "I heard personal testimonies to the sufferings brought on by having to enter the criminal underworld. I had had an abortion, too, but I'd been lucky enough to be in England, where laws were slightly less punishing," Gloria wrote. "I never forgot the weeks of panic before I found a doctor, or how it had changed my life . . . yet I'd never spoken to anyone about this major experience in my life . . . I began to wonder *why* it was illegal; *why* our reproductive lives are not under our own control; and *why* this fundamental issue hadn't been part of any other social justice movement."

One of the hardest things for Gloria to deal with was recognizing her own misconceptions:

All the small humiliations, and . . . even to trust my own experience. For instance, I believed that women couldn't get along with one another, even while my own most trusted friends were women. I had agreed that women were more 'conservative' even while I identified emotionally with every discriminated-against group . . . It is truly amazing how long we can go on accepting myths that oppose our own lives, assuming instead that we are the odd exceptions. But once the light began to dawn, I couldn't understand why I hadn't figured out any of this before.

Chapter Eight

Call Me *Ms.*

Feminism had now become a crusade for Gloria. "It was like the 'testifying' I had heard in southern churches and civil rights meetings of the earlier sixties: emotional, rock-bottom, personal truths," Gloria said. She became a mentor to women writers and, as one writer recalled, she seized the opportunity to open their minds to women's issues: "I used to call her at two or three in the morning, whenever I lost track of whatever I was trying to write, and as she patiently eased me into the next paragraph, she also eased me into feminism's first premise: women are not equal members of human society, and we are not equal because we are women."

Gloria wrote an award-winning article for *New York*: "After Black Power, Women's Liberation." She predicted that if the radical women from the civil rights and peace movements could work with middle-class women from NOW and poor women of all races, "a long-lasting and important mass movement would result."

Male colleagues scoffed at her, wondering why she would jeopardize a hard-won career in serious journalism to write about women. Editors responded to her proposals for articles on the movement with, "Sorry, we published our feminist article last year."

Rather than discourage her, these reactions strengthened her conviction. Each incident brought back memories of her own experience with discrimination:

> . . . the apartments I couldn't get because landlords assumed a single woman couldn't pay the rent (or if she could, she must be a hooker); the political assignments lost to younger and less experienced male writers; the assumption that any work I did get was the result of being a 'pretty girl' (even at a time, I suddenly realized, when all of my editors had been women); the lowered payments because women didn't really need the money; the innuendoes that came along with any recognition ('easier than you think' was how *Newsweek* captioned my photograph as a young writer—a quotation that turned out to be from my own statement that free-lance writing was 'easier than you think'); the well-meaning friends who kept encouraging me to marry any man I was going out with who had talent or money . . .

The pre-feminist Gloria would have ignored these slights, but the new Gloria could not. She began to speak out in public. But what seemed to be a relatively easy task—talking about issues she embraced with groups of mostly like-minded people—became a daunting challenge. Gloria found there was a good reason she preferred to stay behind the scenes writing scripts or reporting on what others said: She was terrified of public speaking.

"It was self-conscious," she recalled. "It was wasteful. I berated myself for this idiotic inability to talk on my own." First, she did not speak at all. Then she tried covering up her fear by quoting facts and statistics, acceptable in writing but the kiss of death in a speech.

Feminist Flo Kennedy came up to her after one such fact-filled bummer and said, "Look, if you're lying in a ditch with a truck on your ankle, you don't send somebody to the library to find out how much the truck weighs. You get it *off.*"

Flo reminded Gloria that she had a grand sense of the absurd and encouraged her to use these talents in public speaking. They began to speak as a pair, and Gloria soon realized that speaking one's heart and one's mind was not only okay, it was more memorable—and more quotable.

Gloria got in trouble more than once for public statements, but on the whole she learned well from Flo. Working with a partner became an essential tool to combat her public-speaking terrors, and she sometimes managed to perform well on late-night talk shows as well as with women's groups. Seeing herself on television for the first time came as a shock. Gloria recalls:

> There was this thin, pretty, blondish woman of medium height who spoke in a boring monotone and, through lack of animation, seemed calm, even blasé in a New York way . . . What I felt *inside* was a

plump brunette from Toledo, too tall and much too pudding-faced, with looks that might be pretty-on-a-good-day but were mostly very ordinary, and a voice that felt constantly on the verge of revealing some unacceptable emotion. I was amazed: Where had this woman on television come from?"

Twenty years later she would ask herself, "Where did that woman in my mind come from?"

Despite her fears and uncertainties, Gloria found herself super-charged after many speaking engagements with women's groups. Once their prepared remarks were out of the way, she and her partner would invite questions and comments from the audience. The response from these early audiences would often ignite a free-wheeling discussion of the issues as they affected those particular women in that particular place. The discussion would lead to the question, *What can we do about it?*, and the answer usually led to action: a protest march, a letter-writing campaign, or a newly-formed local women's group.

These brain-storming sessions were then, and remain today, one of the most meaningful aspects of Gloria's work as a feminist. "I've learned from the collective wisdom of these audiences . . . and people in groups everywhere who are especially valuable as advisers about what I or others could be doing better.

"I've always been hooked on this 'found wisdom,' as I've come to think of it."

By 1970, the feminist movement was growing in

numbers and in influence. It also had plenty of enemies. However, more and more people were beginning to see that discrimination was all too real.

National news magazines such as *Time* and *Newsweek* published lengthy reports on the status of women. The statistics were damning: though one-third of American women worked outside the home, their wages averaged fifty-eight percent of what men earned; male high school graduates earned more than women college graduates; women outranked men only in the numbers living in poverty. *Time* described women's status "as relentlessly second class as . . . any minority."

August 1970 marked the fiftieth anniversary of the 19th Amendment, which guaranteed women's right to vote. Feminists around the country began to organize the first commemorative marches, and Gloria was a key player in the New York effort. She was also writing an article which would have a defining role in her career— a serious opinion piece about the women's movement for a national magazine, *Time*.

In Gloria's essay, "What It Would Be Like If Women Win," she commented on the goals she had in mind:

> Any change is fearful, especially one affecting both politics and sex roles, so let me begin these utopian speculations with a fact . . . Women don't want to exchange places with men . . . That is not our goal. But we do want to change the economic system to one more based on merit . . . In this country, come Utopia, men and women won't reverse roles; they

will be free to choose according to individual talents
and preferences.

Coupled with the media attention she received for
her role in New York's suffrage commemoration march,
"What . . . If Women Win" propelled Gloria into the
spotlight (although she was paid less than men who
wrote in that essay spot). This led to a feature story
about her in *Newsweek*, and though she asked them not
to use her photo on the cover, the magazine found a file
photo from a rally and used it despite Gloria's request.
She became the media's darling and began receiving
much of the attention that she knew should have been
paid to the women who had led the movement from its
infancy. Not surprisingly, many of these women resented her for this attention. This resentment would
continue for many years to come.

While it was perhaps unfair of the media to focus on
Gloria, it was obvious why it happened. She was one of
them—a working journalist with a reputation in the
profession. She was articulate but unpretentious, outspoken without sounding strident or confrontational,
and she could now define the issues without spouting
off lists of boring statistics. She was also funny, unflap-
pable, and highly photogenic. While a few other feminists, such as Betty Friedan, had achieved national
prominence, Gloria was to become a more frequent
spokesperson.

One spin-off from her *Time* essay was Gloria's appearance on David Susskind's television talk show.

Among those watching the program was a Harvard Law School graduate, Brenda Feigen. Brenda's experience at Harvard had been frustrating, demeaning, and just plain wretched. The prevailing attitude was that women students "were taking the place of men who would be breadwinners." But when she saw Gloria on the Susskind show, she said, "This was [my] first realization that what [I'd] been fighting for during those three long years at Cambridge had broader repercussions for the rest of the world."

Brenda began working with NOW's efforts to pass an Equal Rights Amendment. The purpose of the amendment was simple. It stated that no citizen's constitutional rights could be limited because of sex. Brenda and Gloria met during preparations for congressional testimony on the ERA and quickly became friends. NOW's focus on the ERA was critical, but Brenda and Gloria thought there should be a place to help women who did not have time for meetings. They were concerned about day-to-day issues affecting women: job discrimination, violence in the home, and day care. In early 1971, they organized the Women's Action Alliance. Soon, they received mountains of letters from women asking for help and information on how to become involved.

To answer all these questions letter-by-letter would have swamped the tiny organization. Gloria and Brenda began talking about putting together a newsletter. This led to talk of starting a magazine that would be "a feminist forum." Magazines are expensive to start, and they began looking for sources of money. Gloria was getting more paid speaking engagements, and she put most of this money into the magazine.

Gloria was also traveling the country to talk with women's groups about their concerns and to get their ideas about the possibility of a national magazine. Still uncomfortable with public speaking, she always traveled with one of several feminist speaking companions, all African-Americans, whose perspective gave women's issues more relevance to those who were neither white nor middle class. Her travels convinced her the movement was growing. "Despite deprecations the media were then reporting about 'Women's Lib' or 'bra burners' . . . daily rebellions and dreams of equality—inside families and in public life—were sprouting up everywhere," she said.

Gloria was most impressed with what was going on outside the major metropolitan areas: "Rebellion was less rhetorical and more real in parts of the country where women's alternatives were more restricted than in the big cities of New York and California, and at economic levels where women's salaries were even more crucial than among the middle-class rebels who were the focus of the press."

Still, feminism was misrepresented as an angry group of grim-faced man-haters. Gloria's popularity helped to begin changing this image. Gloria's definition of feminism as "the equality and full humanity of women and men" appealed to a wider group of people than some of the earlier feminists. But it made her even more controversial among those early leaders. Activist and author Susan Brownmiller admitted, "I often grew cross as I saw hard-won, original insights developed by others in near total anonymity be turned by the media into Gloria Steinem pronouncements, Gloria Steinem ideas, and Gloria Steinem visions . . ." Other feminists never forgave her.

Gloria was deeply hurt by her critics within the movement, but as she had so many times before, she channeled her pain into positive action. In addition to her work with the Women's Action Alliance, Gloria and Brenda Feigan joined with Betty Friedan, Congresswomen Bella Abzug and Shirley Chisholm (the first black woman elected to the U.S. House of Representatives) to form the National Women's Political Caucus. NWPC brought together feminists from a broad spectrum of groups, including the League of Women Voters and civil rights and civil liberties organizations. NWPC's purpose was to pull women's groups from across political lines, as Gloria explained, to "get pro-equality women of all races into elected and appointed political office."

As the 1972 election drew near, conflict threatened to splinter the NWPC. One faction of the group opposed the inclusion of welfare and abortion rights, as well as stands against racism, in the group's agenda at the 1972 Democratic National Convention.

Betty Friedan led the faction trying to downplay those controversial issues, while Gloria felt they should be included in the debate. Betty began to look on Gloria, Bella and others as rivals who were trying to usurp her leadership. The situation only worsened when Gloria, attempting to prevent the concentration of feminist leadership in the hands of a few, pointed to Betty and Bella, saying, "I'm tired of your face and yours, and I'm tired of seeing my own."

The media portrayed this splintering as a cat fight among feminists and implied that the conflict was yet another example of how women, even in an effort to better their own lives, could not get along. In actuality, the cause of the conflict was more fundamental.

While it is true that Friedan felt personally offended at the amount of media attention Gloria received, and this may have sharpened some of the rhetoric, she was also concerned that Gloria represented a new, and more radical, feminism. Friedan was essentially a liberal reformer. She thought the struggle should focus on issues such as equal pay, affordable child care, and access to education. She also advocated bringing fairness and equality into marriages.

Gloria, however, argued for much more radical changes. She believed that it was impossible for women and men to become full partners because of their unequal power in society. She said that marriage was "a five- or ten-thousand-year-old experiment that we should just declare a failure." Whereas Friedan said that a woman should not have to apologize for devoting herself to her husband and children, Gloria stated: "With homemakers having the highest rate of alcoholism, chemical dependency and depression, the most dangerous place for a woman is in her home." Friedan wanted

Congresswoman Bella Abzug was among the founders of the National Women's Political Caucus, which was formed in 1971. *(Library of Congress)*

to concentrate on making women's lives better within the existing social structure; Gloria advocated a massive reorganization of how men and women interrelate—and said there could be no true equality until this reformation had occurred. Friedan also wanted to focus on heterosexual women's issues, especially those affecting the middle-class, while Gloria saw the movement more expansively, as a liberation movement for oppressed people everywhere.

As the split became more divisive, and public, Friedan began to argue that Gloria and her supporters were as sexist as men—"female chauvinist boors"—and argued that they were inviting a backlash from men. She said that Gloria seemed to think that women were superior merely because they were women. She also made direct attacks on Gloria in the press, even once accusing her of "ripping-off" the women's movement.

At first Gloria responded to Friedan's attacks, but as she realized that their dispute was receiving more media coverage than women's issues, she shifted her focus to starting a feminist magazine that went beyond middle class concerns. There was no shortage of experienced women who were eager to write, and by late 1971 Gloria and a team of journalists and editors had compiled 130 pages of articles by and for the new feminist audience. This was a unique chance, said Lindsy Van Gelder, "to practice journalism with feminism as a given."

The articles were edited, but they had still not been able to raise enough money to go to press. Then Gloria's old friend and colleague Clay Felker offered to publish a thirty-page sample as an insert in *New York*'s annual double issue in December 1972. They all agreed that the sample would focus on many issues of what Clay called "the contagion of feminism."

A mad scramble ensued to get the preview ready, but they still needed a name. "Sisters" was Gloria's favorite until Catholic women said they thought it sounded like a magazine about nuns. "Sojourner" came next, after abolitionist and suffragist Sojourner Truth, but that was scrapped when others pointed out that it sounded like a travel magazine.

Then "Ms." was suggested. At the time Ms. was used by some feminists who objected to a woman's courtesy title being linked to her marital status, unlike the man's title "Mr." Gloria did some research and found that Ms. had been used as an alternative in secretarial handbooks for women whose marital status was not known. The new magazine had a name.

The *Ms.* insert in *New York* was a success. Volunteers came forward to help on everything from budget planning to incorporation. Donors who just months earlier had refused to open their checkbooks for *Ms.* quickly changed their minds. Katherine Graham, owner of the *Washington Post*, was the first to come through with a major investment—$20,000—and others soon followed.

Ms.'s 120-page Spring 1972 Preview issue sold out 300,000 copies in eight days. Within a few weeks the staff had received over 20,000 letters and 26,000 subscription orders.

Chapter Nine

CLICK!

The debut of *Ms.* brought Gloria an onslaught of speaking and interview requests, which she both welcomed and dreaded. She wanted more than ever to speak to groups about feminist issues, but she still had not conquered her fear of public speaking. Teaming up with Flo Kennedy, child-care advocate Dorothy Pitman Hughes, and civil rights activist Margaret Sloan helped her get through the times when her mouth dried up and her knees wobbled. All three speaking partners were eloquent and insightful. To Gloria's great delight, audiences from Wichita to Walla Walla to Washington, D.C. began discussing the issues and how they related to their personal and local concerns. In an almost magical way, she said, "the audience takes over and creates its own organizing meeting."

Her forays into media interviews were much less fulfilling. For one thing, she was not prepared for the amount of attention paid to her looks, or, as she said, "finding myself referred to as 'the pretty one.' Rationally, I knew it was a response of surprise, based on what the media thought feminists looked like (if a woman could get a man, why would she need equal pay?), and this was especially clear to me because I was judged much prettier *after* I was identified as a feminist than I ever had been *before*."

She tried to play down her looks, ditching her miniskirts and makeup, letting her hair fall naturally from a part in the middle (though she continued to wear it streaked), and donning what unintentionally became her trademark aviator glasses. It did not work. Interviewers persisted in veering away from the issues and instead wanted to focus on her personal life—from whom she was dating to how her apartment was decorated. Gloria was determined to get as much publicity for the women's movement as possible, but more and more she found herself canceling interviews at the last minute.

Even so, Gloria was in a whirlwind of activity that set her pace for the next thirty years. She was very busy with *Ms.*—finding and meeting with writers and editors and assigning articles, trying to appeal to advertisers, and keeping the bills paid. But speaking engagements were also high on her list of priorities, as were organizing support for the Equal Rights Amendment and working with the National Women's Political Caucus. She rarely said no to anyone.

Ms. was a dramatic change from any women's magazine then in publication. Instead of focusing on fashion and homemaking as other women's magazines did, *Ms.* published articles devoted to more serious political, social, and philosophical issues facing women. Determined to give reproductive rights a major presence in *Ms.*, for example, the editors kicked off with a declaration addressed to Congress and state legislatures. "We Have Had Abortions" was signed by fifty-three well-known women, including Gloria, tennis great Billie Jean King, singer Judy Collins, and writer Lillian Hellman.

One of the writers Gloria had solicited for the Preview issue was her friend Jane O'Reilly. Although Jane still had some reservations about feminism, she was skilled at getting a laugh out of the most complex of issues. Gloria asked her to write on "housework," since Jane was then a stay-at-home mom as well as an accomplished writer. Jane later joked that housework "was the only subject in the movement inventory I felt qualified to address."

Once Jane got into it, though, "I began to grasp that *waiting* for equality might not be the most effective political tool. It took me three months to write 'Click! The Housewife's Moment of Truth' and when I finished I had become a wild-eyed radical libber—a woman people edged away from at social gatherings."

Jane's article became a classic, and "Click!" became the by-word of women throughout the country. Her examples were indeed moments of truth:

> . . . a friend of mine stood and watched her husband step over a pile of toys on the stairs, put there to be carried up. 'Why can't you get this stuff put away?'

he mumbled. Click! 'You have two hands,' she said, turning away.

On Fire Island my weekend hostess and I had just finished cooking breakfast, lunch, and washing dishes for both. A male guest came wandering into the kitchen just as the last dish was being put away and said, 'How about something to eat?' He sat down expectantly and started to read the paper. Click! 'You work all week,' said the hostess, 'and *I* work all week, and if you want something to eat, you can get it, and wash up after yourself.

Readers everywhere copied the article, passed it around in offices, used it as a topic of discussion, and mailed it to like-minded friends and family. For the next few years, many men stood by in bafflement as women nudged each other with a wink and said "Click!"

Many of them wrote to *Ms.*, describing incidents in which a Click! emboldened them to stand up for themselves. For the *Ms.* crew, Letters to the Editor became the plum in the pudding. Gloria remembers "reading at random from bulging mailbags that brought a total of twenty thousand letters to our one-room office. I remembered many, many women who said they felt 'crazy' or 'alone' until they found *Ms.* on their newsstands . . . Some said they had asked their husbands to read *Ms.* and felt it helped their marriage. Others said it had given them the courage to leave."

The letters gave the *Ms.* staff courage in return. Despite the fledgling magazine's statistical success, going forward with such an ambitious project was terrifying at times, especially fund-raising and trying to find advertisers who shared *Ms.*'s belief that American women were eager for a magazine that spoke about the issues that concerned them, not just recipes and diet tips. The staff drew strength, said Gloria, from "reading the words of generous, time-giving readers who keep us connected, accountable, and on the cutting edge of change."

As fast as subscriptions and small donations were coming in, the staff and volunteers knew all too well that it would take years of constant fund-raising to make the magazine self-sustaining. In effect, they had to make *Ms.* a long-term success before the first regular issue rolled off the press. They raised the money they needed in a breakneck effort by making phone calls and writing letters, and in face-to-face solicitations, darting from cab to cab across the city and plane to plane across the country.

The first monthly issue of *Ms.* was published in July 1972 to an enthusiastic reception, far beyond the founders' most hopeful predictions. The Letters column grew into pages of intimate discussions between readers. Readers talked of their own successes and failures, of doubt and inspiration, and they brought serious attention to age-old problems, such as battering and sexual harassment, which had been taken for granted for so long they did not even have names.

The women's movement was on a roll, its influence felt from the American household to the U.S. Supreme Court. The Court was then considering the legal arguments in two cases that were to become landmarks for women's rights: *Roe v. Wade* and *Doe v. Bolton*, both arguing that women have a constitutional right to abortion. There were already a host of cases in the federal courts brought by doctors challenging the criminal penalties for performing abortions. By choosing *Roe* and *Doe* to test the issue, the Supreme Court indicated that the justices wanted to focus on women's rights, not criminal law.

The 1972 Democratic National Convention, held shortly after *Ms.* premiered, demonstrated how far the women's movement had come. Thanks to reform rules following the 1968 convention in Chicago, women made up forty percent of the 1972 delegates, and women's issues, including abortion, were included in the party's platform. Although George McGovern was defeated by the incumbent president, Richard Nixon, in a landslide, women's rights advocates had put their issues on the national stage.

While feminists turned their hope to the Supreme Court's forthcoming decision on *Roe* and *Doe*, one of the articles Gloria wrote for *Ms.* was on a most unlikely subject: Marilyn Monroe. If anyone appeared to be the antithesis of the women's movement, it was this icon of movie star sexuality who had died in 1962.

Gloria cherished the hours she had spent at the movies as a child, when she needed refuge from her responsibilities to her mother. But she had been embarrassed by Marilyn Monroe and actually walked out on her films. "I remember her on the screen, huge as a colossus doll, mincing and whispering and hoping her way into total vulnerability," she said. "Watching her, I felt angry, even humiliated, but I didn't understand why."

Gloria later realized that she resented Marilyn for exposing "the neediness that so many women feel, but try so hard to hide . . . How dare she, a movie star, be just as unconfident as I was?"

She began to see that Marilyn had been made into a caricature, a ditzy air head, not unlike the Bunny image that Gloria had written about years before. Gloria also felt close to Monroe because they shared similar childhood experiences.

In her article, "The Woman Who Died Too Young," Gloria took a serious, generous, and courageous look at Marilyn Monroe. Gloria discovered that Monroe had stood up for black artists in the 1950s when they were banned from getting bookings in most major night clubs. Monroe personally phoned the manager of a Los Angeles club, telling him that if he hired Ella Fitzgerald, she would take a front row seat at every performance. The legendary jazz singer was hired, and Marilyn kept her promise.

Marilyn also stood up to the powerful Hollywood studios when they threatened to blackball her if she married Arthur Miller, who was at the time being hounded as a communist sympathizer by the infamous House Un-American Activities Committee. Miller had refused to cooperate with the committee and gained national acclaim for his bravery, but Marilyn's courageous choice to marry him and risk her career received barely a mention.

Gloria found a quote from what turned out to be Marilyn's last interview. In it, Marilyn pleads with the reporter to focus on "what I really want to say: That what the world really needs is a real feeling of kinship. Everybody: stars, laborers, Negroes, Jews, Arabs. We are all brothers . . . Please don't make me a joke. End the interview with what I believe."

That kind of article made *Ms.* unique. Here was a feminist magazine that was neither boringly academic nor packed with movement rhetoric. It was unpredictable. It often inspired readers to take action and, most importantly, to think.

Respect for *Ms.* was far from universal, though. Some men wrote angry letters accusing *Ms.* of everything from breaking up their homes to advocating castration. Others dismissed it as the rantings of silly women. Harry Reasoner, the veteran TV news reporter, said, "I'll give it six months before they run out of things to say." Columnist James J. Kilpatrick likened *Ms.* to "C-sharp on an untuned piano. [*Ms.*] is a note of petulance, of bitchiness, or nervous fingernails screeching across a blackboard."

The hostility of critics was at times hurtful, but for Gloria and most *Ms.* supporters, the criticism meant one thing: neither *Ms.* nor the women's movement could be ignored. A window to equality was open, if not yet the door.

Chapter Ten

Trashing

In 1972, *Ms.* set up the non-profit Ms. Foundation for Women to raise money to benefit women's causes in the areas of employment, reproductive health, violence against women, and girl's issues. Gloria also donated much of her outside income from speaking and writing to women's groups she encountered as she traveled.

She was increasingly in the limelight as a spokesperson for the women's movement. *McCall's* named Gloria "Woman of the Year," she was on the cover of *New Woman*, and was interviewed in *Redbook*. She addressed the National Press Club—the first woman to do so— and made occasional appearances on TV and radio to discuss specific issues.

The media attention was a blessing because Gloria could address women's issues on a national scale, but it was also a curse, for Gloria became a lightning rod for critics, feminists as well as anti-feminists.

Many feminists who had predated her in the movement were still resentful of how the media focused on her. From their point of view they had done the early work, raising the issues and bringing the movement to the point where it began to take hold. Then came this glamorous newcomer who stole their thunder and reaped their glory. They called her a lightweight opportunist who used her rich-and-famous cohorts to climb to the top, and they predicted she would drop the movement when she got bored or got tired of *real* work. They also accused her of manipulating her way into the lives of powerful men in order to boost her own career.

Betty Friedan remained Gloria's most vocal critic. As late as 1970, Betty was labeled the "Mother Superior of Women's Lib," a title that she cherished. Friedan had strong views about what were and what were not feminist issues. She attacked issues she did not agree with, such as lesbian rights, and feminists who supported them, such as Gloria, by calling them "man-hating radicals."

Gloria had tolerated Friedan's hostility toward her for years because she refused to jeopardize her reputation, and the movement's, by going on the defensive. Most of her critics interpreted her silence as aloofness, but by refusing to respond she was also hiding a great deal of pain.

As much as these attacks hurt Gloria, she was more concerned about the effect the media attention had on her mother. Ruth had made tremendous strides in her recovery from mental illness—moving to her own apartment, making friends, taking classes, getting a part-time job, and joining a multi-racial Episcopal church that worked with the poor and homeless and had a woman priest. She still had periods when the old terrors came back, but on the whole she was functioning well.

Gloria would plead with reporters to leave Ruth alone, but Ruth's history was too hard to resist. Reports about Ruth and Gloria living adjacent to the furnace room, having a derelict rat-infested house, or of how Gloria had to become her mother's caretaker, sent Ruth into an emotional tailspin.

It took the breaking of the Watergate story—that the Nixon administration was behind the burglary of the Democratic Party headquarters during the 1972 presidential elections, and the resulting inquiries that ultimately drove the president from office—to divert the media's attention. Major stories about women's issues began to seem more important than Gloria Steinem's background as well.

In January 1973, the U.S. Supreme Court announced its historic decision in *Roe v. Wade.* The majority of justices held that the 14th Amendment and the inherent right to privacy implicit in the U.S. Constitution secured abortion as a personal issue between a woman and her doctor that was outside the strictures of various state and federal laws. States had no constitutional authority to interfere in such a personal matter. (They did, however, decide that once the fetus became viable, at about six months in the womb, states could prohibit abortion "except when it is necessary . . . for the preservation of the life or health of the mother.")

The Equal Rights Amendment looked like a sure winner too. This proposed amendment consisting of one simple statement—*Equality of rights shall not be denied or abridged by the United States or any state on account of sex*—had easily passed in both houses of Congress in 1972 and was sent to the states for ratification. By 1974, thirty-three of the required thirty-eight states had ratified it. The women's movement seemed to be riding an unstoppable wave.

Ms. was making waves of its own, and occasionally it created problems for Gloria. One of the editors remembered that although most people at the magazine shared Steinem's views on major issues, such as abortion rights, there were feminists who disagreed with her. Dealing with these divisions within the movement took all of Gloria's political skills.

Leading supporters of the Equal Rights Amendment march in Washington in 1978, urging Congress to extend the time for ratification of the ERA. From left: Bella Abzug, Gloria Steinem, Dick Gregory, Betty Friedan, and Representatives Barbara Mikulski and Margaret Heckler. *(AP Photo/Dennis Cook)*

A more immediate and visible problem with *Ms.* was the lack of advertising. Gloria had not realized the degree to which national advertisers held women's magazines to a different standard than general publications. Food products companies, for example, might pull their ads from a general interest magazine that runs an article criticizing their product. But women's magazines are denied ads *unless* they agree to feature or editorially praise those products—a cheese ad would have to be placed on the page facing an article on "100 Ways to Make Macaroni"—while there is no such requirement for *People Magazine*. *Ms.* had to work extra hard to find advertisers that would comply with its own views and those of its supporters.

Gloria and publisher Patricia Carbine, who left a top-level position at *McCall's* to head *Ms.*, were the early ad sales staff. They were always a curiosity when they called on corporations soliciting advertisements. People would ogle from their office doors or wander into sales meetings. "They looked at us like we were Martians," said *Ms.*'s first ad sales manager. ". . . it was very tough on the ego. They would not take us—or the magazine—seriously."

Gloria was on the go constantly, somehow balancing her work with *Ms.*, which was more than a full-time job, with speaking and organizing. She continued to use the organizing skills she had learned with the Gandhians in India—watch, listen, learn.

But Gloria missed being able to follow her other passion—writing. She had initially made a two-year commitment to *Ms.*, thinking that once it was off the ground she could go back to freelancing. By the mid-1970s she realized that she was now considered a "one-issue" writer. No other magazines would work with her on stories outside the women's movement.

Nineteen seventy-five was a difficult year for Gloria. Her mother's mental state was in decline again. The energetic, self-reliant woman Gloria had just begun to know—the woman who played touch football with Susanne's kids—was becoming bitter and fearful. Ruth had her own apartment within Susanne's home, with a paid companion to tend to her. But when Susanne decided, at age fifty, to go to law school, Ruth became unreasonable. She complained that theirs was no longer a *real* family, there was no love, no home-cooked food. At one point she threatened to call the *New York Times* to "tell them that this was what feminism did: it left old sick women all alone." Eventually, Gloria and Susanne were compelled to put Ruth in a nursing home. Despite round-the-clock care and attentive nurses, Ruth continued to decline in spirit and in health.

At the same time, Gloria and *Ms.* were publicly accused of being operatives of the CIA. By 1975 the nation was reeling from the exposure of the Nixon Administration's role in the Watergate conspiracy, as well as revelations about the Federal Bureau of Investigation's (FBI) attempted sabotage of the civil rights and anti-war movements, and of the Central Intelligence Agency's secret actions against citizens and governments around the world. At this time to even hint that a movement's leader, such as Gloria, had secret connections to the FBI or the CIA was enough to destroy her credibility.

Some members of the then-defunct Redstockings, the feminists whose abortion speak-out spurred Gloria to activism, charged that "Gloria Steinem has a ten-year association with the CIA stretching from 1959 to 1969 which she has misrepresented and covered up. Furthermore, we have become convinced that *Ms.* magazine, founded and edited by her, is hurting the women's liberation movement."

The charges centered mostly around her work in the late 1950s for the Communist Youth Conference in Vienna. Although Gloria had learned that the CIA had funded the Independent Research Service, she had done nothing to further the actions of the agency. Stunned and deeply hurt, Gloria knew that if she took a public stance to counter the charges she might spark a national controversy. Her silence on the charges, however, raised even more suspicion among activists and *Ms.* readers who flooded the magazine's phone lines to get Gloria's side of the story. She remained silent throughout that summer, sustained by her close friends and the *Ms.* staff, who tried to assure her that this would blow over.

Many feminists were bewildered by Gloria's refusal to respond to the charges. After much soul-searching and much more discussion, Gloria gave in and wrote a six-page, single-spaced letter to the feminist press about the Independent Research Service:

I took no orders at all from the U.S. government in any of its forms or agencies. For better or worse, I have always been my own person. I naively believed that the ultimate money source didn't matter, since no control or orders came with it. It's painfully clear with hindsight that even indirect, control-free funding was a mistake but I didn't realize it then.

As Gloria had feared, her reply caught the attention of a *New York Times* reporter who then wrote about the controversy. "Dissension Among Feminists: The Rift Widens" was given three-quarters of a page in a prominent section of the *Times*, and then it was syndicated nationally. The *Washington Post* also ran a nationally syndicated story, focusing on the Redstockings' charges and other attacks on Gloria. The *Post*'s conclusion that "the *Ms.* myth is waning" made advertisers take note.

Gloria refused to be deterred by the controversy and soon was included among the leaders of the historic 1977 National Women's Conference, an outgrowth of the 1975 International Women's Year Conference in Mexico City.

In the meantime, however, opponents to feminist issues had developed a national force of their own. Phyllis Schlafly's Eagle Forum and other conservative religious and political leaders began to organize against the Equal Rights Amendment. They charged that the ERA would destroy the family, draft women into military combat, and lead to unisex restrooms. They charged that abortion was a mortal crime, not a right, and should be banned.

At first many feminists thought their opponents' arguments were so ludicrous that no one would pay attention. But the tide of popular opinion began shifting, and by 1979 the anti-feminists had coalesced into a potent political force.

As the seventies came to a close, *Ms.*'s financial condition was so grim that in desperation Gloria had gone to Katharine Graham, publisher of the *Washington Post*, to see if the paper was interested in buying *Ms.* Katharine had to warn her that any sale, even to the *Post*, would likely turn *Ms.* from a feminist to a more traditional women's magazine filled with the kind of food and fashion features that advertisers required.

After much soul-searching, the *Ms.* founders decided to change the magazine to a non-profit publication. This enabled the foundation to apply for grants and tax-deductible donations to pay the magazine's expenses, thus decreasing its dependence on ad revenue and subscriptions. The first foundation grant for *Ms.* came from the owner and publisher of the *New York Post*, who gave $300,000. This qualified *Ms.* for a matching grant from the Ford Foundation and pulled the magazine from the brink of extinction.

The early 1980s was a difficult time for Gloria personally and for feminism in general. Dealing with the personal attacks from both inside and outside the movement, struggling to keep *Ms.* afloat, fighting with the religious and social conservatives that gained prominence as Republican Ronald Reagan assumed the presidency, taxed every ounce of her physical and emotional strength.

Chapter Eleven

Revolution from Within

Once *Ms.* was financially stable, Gloria ignored how tired she was and went back to her old whirlwind activities. "I believed so little in my own inner world, that I couldn't stop to replenish it. Like a soldier who is wounded but won't lie down for fear of dying, I just kept marching. Why? Well, if I stopped, I would have given up the way I made myself 'real'—that is, by being useful to people in the outside world—just as I had made myself 'real' as a child by keeping so busy that I numbed the sad reality at home where I looked after my mother," wrote Gloria.

By 1981, Ruth Steinem's life was nearing its end. Gloria and Susanne spent time at Ruth's side during her final days, talking and comforting her. When Ruth died in July 1981, Gloria was filled with guilt. She felt that she had not done enough for her mother.

Gloria had always wanted to write about her personal life but had not done so because she knew it would hurt Ruth. "While she was alive, I couldn't talk about any but the most routine, sanitized, good-news parts of our life together," she recalled. "(T)here was also her reluctance to admit that we had ever been poor . . . so a great deal of life was off limits."

Within a few months after her mother's death, Gloria began putting her memories on paper. Throughout her career, writing had not come quickly or easily—it was hard work. But for the essay called "Ruth's Song," the words, the structure, the flow "seemed already to exist," Gloria said. Once it was written, though, Gloria could not bear to read it. It was just too painful.

In 1983, Gloria had a book contract and she decided to include "Ruth's Song (Because She Could Not Sing It)" in a collection of twenty-eight of her essays. She entitled the book *Outrageous Acts and Everyday Rebellions*. Also included were her articles, "I Was a Playboy Bunny" from *Show* and "Marilyn Monroe: The Woman Who Died Too Young." The book contained other articles showing the full range of Gloria's writing talent, such as "If Men Could Menstruate" and "In Praise of Women's Bodies."

Outrageous Acts was a success. The power and poignancy of "Ruth's Song," in particular, struck a chord with readers and enabled Gloria to come to terms with some of the truths of her childhood. This did nothing to slow her down, however. Book signings were piggybacked with fundraisers for *Ms.* and local feminist groups.

As groups such as the Moral Majority, a conservative political group started by religious fundamentalist Reverend Jerry Falwell, became more powerful, newsstands and libraries were urged to ban *Ms.*, and advertisers were pressured to pull ads. This pressure, combined with ever-rising printing and mailing costs, put *Ms.* back in the red. But once Gloria made a commitment, she was not about to give up just because it was difficult. The magazine was caught in a spiral, though. The more money it lost, the harder Gloria and Patricia Carbine had to raise money; the more they traveled looking for contributions, the less time they could spend editing the magazine.

Then Gloria discovered she had breast cancer. Tests showed the tumor was quite small and had not invaded the lymph system, but Gloria remembers feeling outside of herself when she heard the diagnosis. She thought to herself, "Isn't this interesting. So this is how it's going to end." She responded to the diagnosis much as she had responded to other critical situations in her past: she investigated new treatments for her stage of cancer and found a Boston specialist who was a pioneer in lumpectomy, at the time a relatively new procedure in which only the cancerous tissue is removed, rather than taking the entire breast, lymph nodes and underlying muscle, as in a partial or radical mastectomy. She told only her most trusted friends about the surgery. She was so concerned that news of her cancer might further damage *Ms.* that she had checked into the hospital under her old alias, Marie Ochs. Following the surgery and a two-day hospital stay, Gloria returned to New York where she underwent another six weeks of radiation therapy.

Gloria was now teetering on the edge of emotional breakdown. She was bone-weary, and her professional and personal lives were on the verge of collapse. Her friends had been urging her for several years to get into counseling, and in May of 1986 she was finally persuaded to see a female therapist. Gloria's understanding of her situation came almost immediately: She had to offer herself the same dedicated care she gave to everyone else.

Gloria began to make some fundamental changes while in therapy. One of her first moves was to redecorate her apartment from merely a place to hang her clothes and keep her files into a real home, with curtains and dishes and furniture that gave her a feeling of comfort and sanctuary.

As the struggle for *Ms.* was beginning to seem hopeless, two Australian journalists appeared wanting to buy the magazine. They promised not to turn it into a traditional women's magazine; it would stay true to its feminist advocacy. The day *Ms.* passed into Australian hands was a day of relief and mourning. The staff felt relieved that *Ms.* would remain staunchly feminist and they were happy to let go of what had become an impossible burden. At the same time, however, this was a magazine they had nurtured from infancy, through years of joy and heartache, and some were sad to step aside.

As she entered her late fifties, Gloria began to slow down, although her pace would still leave most younger women breathless. She still traveled to speaking engagements and to work with women's groups, but she

In the mid-1980s, Gloria Steinem and the founders of *Ms.* sold the magazine to a pair of Australian journalists who vowed to uphold the publication's feminist roots. *(AP Photos)*

was not on the road or in the air every week, as she had been. She was eating a healthy diet, sleeping regularly, and she had begun an exercise regimen.

Gloria was also continuing work with her therapist. However, one of her most enlightening moments came during a hypnosis session she undertook as research for a new book. She was instructed to let an image of herself as a child emerge. The child she saw was five or six, lying in Gloria's bed at Clark Lake. "She feels relaxed and poured out like molasses," Gloria said.

The feeling of tiredness after a rambunctious day, the sense that this child was not self-conscious but was sure of herself and her body, gave the adult Gloria a reason to smile. At the same time, Gloria recalled, "It was odd to discover this untamed and spontaneous child, someone who existed before the terrifying years of living alone with my mother, and who was shut out when I built a wall to protect me from remembering what happened a few years later. She is so much more physical, confident, and true to herself than I am."

Her years of therapy, of awakening to herself, had given Gloria the inspiration to write another book. *Revolution from Within: A Book on Self-Esteem* was published in 1992. She wrote of her own experiences, but paid more attention to how women can unlearn old patterns and learn new ones that enhance self-esteem.

The news media wasted no opportunity to chortle: *Gloria Steinem has self-esteem problems!* or *Midlife Crisis for Gloria?!* Some simply dismissed the book as New Age nonsense. But it was a hit with readers. People waited in line for hours at her book signings, and many more wrote letters telling Gloria what a difference the book made in their own lives. They understood on her statement, "I finally began to admit that I, too, was more aware of other people's feelings than my own."

Readers also found a mixture of comfort and inspiration in Gloria's adopted mantra: *There is always one true inner voice. Trust it.*

On March 25, 1994, Gloria turned sixty. At the end of her forties, Gloria had used Dante's words to describe her feelings: "a shadowed forest . . . dense and difficult." At fifty, she remembers being in denial, the first stage of aging: "I was going to live exactly as I always had—and make a virtue of it . . . After all, the world could use a pioneer dirty old lady."

Her defiance started to change to excitement at entering a new phase of life. "A friend sent me a photograph of a very old and wonderfully radiant Chinese woman, which I still have posted on my kitchen wall," Gloria said. "She was in a park in the early morning doing tai chi and singing opera. This woman had lots of wrinkles, a gorgeous, beatific smile, and a lilac kerchief. She looked happy, wise, mischievous, and peaceful. She was absolutely beautiful. The moment I saw her I felt, 'This is the person I want to grow into.' "

In many ways, Gloria has grown into that woman, minus some of the wrinkles, plus an aura of serenity. However, when *Ms.* suspended publication in 1998 (it had changed hands more than once following the sale to the Australian women), Gloria again went to work for the magazine, tapping into a network of women to form a feminist consortium, Liberty Media for Women, LLC, which purchased *Ms.* Now published bimonthly, but still distributed through subscriptions and select newsstands, the magazine is once again solidly in the hands of its founders.

Looking back at more frenetic decades, Gloria is filled with a sense of wonder and gratitude: "What I remember most about those years was being flooded with the frequent feeling: *If I'd done only this in my life and nothing more, it would have been enough.* Each day, I thought the next couldn't possibly be more intense and satisfying—and then it was."

Gloria's life has been proof that a woman can be happy and fulfilled as a single woman. She has not insisted that other women live as she does, but she has stated in countless ways over the years that marriage was simply not for her.

Thus, many people were a bit startled when on Labor Day weekend in 2000, Gloria married David Bale, a fifty-nine-year old South African-born anti-apartheid activist, entrepreneur, and single parent of three children. They met a year earlier at a benefit for one of the many organizations Gloria helped found—Voters for Choice. "We're calling it a 'partnership,' " she later said. "He says he feels like he's known me for 30 years, because he's known my work."

"Thirty years of the women's movement," she added, "had changed the marriage laws and made an equal marriage possible."

And in a statement to the Associated Press she said, "I'm happy, surprised and one day will write about it, but for now, I hope this proves what feminists have always said—that feminism is about the ability to choose what's right at each time of our lives."

A few weeks later, before a standing-room-only crowd gathered for her speech on a college campus, Gloria was relaxed and light-hearted. She wore little makeup and dressed simply in black trousers and a knit top. After her introduction, Gloria gave a huge hug to the student who organized the event, took the microphone, and asked the audience to turn their applause to the sparkly-eyed student.

Gloria kept her prepared remarks brief in order to give the audience a chance for questions. If the old magic happened, she told them, the event would turn into an organizational meeting.

The questioning was lively, but no one seemed to want to take the next step: defining the issues for that particular campus in that particular town. That was all right with Gloria—sometimes it happened and some-times it did not. Only time would tell whether someone walked out of the auditorium with a spark that would one day ignite and turn her into the next generation's Gloria Steinem.

Sources

Chapter One: Heritage

p. 9, "who taught me to love . . ." and "who performed . . ." Gloria Steinem, *Outrageous Acts and Everyday Rebellions* (New York: Holt, Rhinehart and Winston, 1983,) Dedication.

p. 12, "We are responsible . . ." American Theosophical Society, "Some Concepts of Theosophy," (http://members.aol.com/tstec/hmpage/tsideas.htm)

p. 12, "most important inheritances." Carolyn G. Heilbrun, *The Education of a Woman: The Life of Gloria Steinem.* (New York: The Dial Press, Bantam Doubleday Dell Publishing Group, 1995,) 8.

p. 13, "the best-paid job . . ." Ibid., 13.

p. 13, "a resort worthy . . ." Steinem, *Outrageous Acts*, 132.

p. 15, "breaking point" and "From now on . . ." Ibid., 138.

Chapter Two: A Child's Worst Fears

p. 17, "Doc Howard's . . ." Steinem, *Outrageous Acts*, 132.

p. 17, "through the entirety . . ." Heilbrun, *Education*, 46.

p. 17, "Louisa May Alcott . . ." Ibid., 29.

p. 17, "He treated me . . ." Ibid., 20.

p. 17, ". . . a great time of running wild . . ." Ibid., 16,

p. 18, "was of brushing her hair . . ." Gloria Steinem, *Revolution From Within: A Book of Self-Esteem* (Boston: Little, Brown and Company, 1992,) 236.

p. 21, "I remember so well . . ." Ibid., 92.

p. 22, "Women were so clearly divided . . ." Heilbrun, *Education,* 27.

p. 22, "I always knew . . ." Ibid., 24.

p. 23, "All right . . ." Ibid., 31.

Chapter Three: Independence

p. 25, "We've just finished . . ." Heilbrun, *Education*, 47.

p. 25, "I had so little experience . . ." Ibid., 51.

p. 25, "Don't worry . . ." Ibid.

p. 25, "When you spoke to her . . ." Ibid., 48.

p. 26, "Why study . . ." Ibid., 64

p. 26, "At this moment . . ." Ibid., 60.

p. 28, "she promise to do . . ." Ibid., 68.

p. 28, "the mysterious East . . ." Ibid., 71.

p. 28, "I discovered . . ." Gloria Steinem, *Moving Beyond Words* (New York: Simon & Schuster, 1994) 264.

p. 29, "to be respected as one . . ." Ibid., 73.

p. 29, "Instead of weapons . . ." Ibid., 265.

p. 30, "[W]e walked . . ." Ibid., 265.

p. 30, "If you do something . . ." Ibid., 266.

p. 30, "Most of us have . . ." Ibid., 266.

Chapter Four: Writer and Activist

p. 32, "The educational shame was this . . ." Steinem, *Revolution*, 118.

p. 32, "were the nineteenth century . . ." Ibid., 118.

p. 33, "overqualified . . ." Heilbrun, *Education*, 84.

p. 34, "remembers feeling relief . . ." Ibid., 84.

p. 34, "I think it struck a lot of us . . ." Ibid., 89.

p. 35, "When we arrived . . ." Ibid., 89.

p. 36, "For me, writing is . . ." Steinem, *Outrageous Acts*, 12.

p. 38, "chutzpah." Heilbrun, *Education,* 92.

Chapter Five: Awakening

p. 40, "I shared the reaction . . ." Steinem, *Moving*, 269.

p. 41, "identified with the poor . . ." Steinem, *Revolution*. 234.

p. 41, "satisfyingly unladylike" and "patched myself . . ." Ibid., 234.

p. 42, "The whole costume . . ." Ibid., 37.

p. 42, "the vault . . ." Ibid., 37.

p. 44, "Two hundred dollars . . ." Ibid., 53.

p. 44, "Somehow, the usual . . ." Ibid., 65.

p. 45, "It was still one of the . . ." Heilbrun., 106.

p. 45, "trying on the name and life . . ." Steinem, *Revolution*, 263.

p. 45, "I'll definitely get married . . ." Ibid., 263.

p. 46, "that was the way . . ." Ibid., 38.

Chapter Six: The Road to Feminism

p. 48, "Apparently . . . the appearance . . ." Steinem, *Outrageous Acts*, 88.

p. 48, "Feminist ideas began . . ." Steinem, *Revolution*. 234.

p. 48, "feeling we couldn't go . . ." Ibid., 234.

p. 49, "For the first time . . ." Steinem, *Outrageous Acts*, 17.

Chapter Seven: Breakthrough

p. 53, "learned to Uncle Tom . . ." Steinem, *Outrageous Acts,* 113.

p. 53, "My work won't interfere . . ." Ibid., 113.

p. 54, "There seems to be no punishment . . ." Ibid., 117.

p. 54, "unescorted ladies . . ." Steinem, *Revolution*, 22.

p. 54, "I was humiliated . . ." Ibid., 23.

p. 55, "Sure enough, the manager . . ." Ibid., 23.

p. 55, "When I faced the hotel manager again . . ." Ibid., 25.

p. 55, "no broads." Steinem, *Outrageous Acts*, 102.

p. 55, "raised as much money . . ." Ibid., 100.

p. 56, "I think it's precisely *because* . . ." Ibid., 102.

p. 56, "have a celebration . . ." Heilbrun, *Education,* 156.

p. 58, "To deny women birth control . . ." Ibid., 157.

p. 59, "I heard personal testimonies . . ." Steinem, *Moving*, 269.

p. 60, "all the small humiliations . . ." Heilbrun, *Education*, 171.

Chapter Eight: Call Me *Ms.*

p. 61, "It was like 'testifying'. . ." Steinem, *Outrageous Acts*, 17.

p. 61, "I used to call her . . ." Jane O'Reilly, *The Girl I Left Behind: The Housewife's Moment of Truth and Other Feminist Ravings* (New York: Macmillan Publishing Co., Inc., 1980,) xi.

p. 61, "a long-lasting . . ." Ibid., 18.

p. 62, "Sorry, we published . . ." Ibid., 19.

p. 62, ". . . the apartments I couldn't get . . ." Ibid., 18.

p. 63, "It was self-conscious . . ." Ibid., 9.

p. 63, "Look, if you're lying . . ." Ibid., 9.

p. 63, "There was this thin, pretty . . ." Steinem, *Revolution*, 227.

p. 64, "I've learned from the collective . . ." Steinem, *Moving*, 271.

p. 65, "as relentlessly second class . . ." *Time* Archives, "Who's' Come A Long Way, Baby?", www.time.com/time/magazine/1998/dom/980629/cover_related.html, Aug. 31, 1970. 2.

p. 65, "Any change is fearful . . ." Gloria Steinem, "What It Would Be Like If Women Win," *Time* Capsule, *Time* Education Program, www.time.com/time/teach/archive/000424/test5.html, Aug. 31, 1970.

p. 67, "were taking the place of men . . ." Heilbrun, *Education*, 206.

p. 67, "This was [my] first . . ." Ibid., 207.

p. 68, "Despite deprecations . . ." Steinem, *Outrageous Acts*, 2.

p. 68, "Rebellion was less rhetorical . . ." Ibid., 2.

p. 68, "the equality and . . ." Ibid., 3.

p. 69, ". . . I often grew cross . . ." Ibid., 165.

p. 69, "get pro-equality women . . ." Author's correspondence, June 16, 2001.

p. 70, "I'm tired of your face . . ." Heilbrun, *Education,* 214.

p. 72, "to practice journalism . . ." "*Ms.* Herstory," *Ms.* Online, www.msmagazine,com/msherstory.html, 2000.

p. 73, "the contagion of feminism." Heilbrun, *Education,* 219.

Chapter Nine: *CLICK!*

p. 74, "the audience takes over . . ." Steinem, *Moving*, 271.

p. 74, "finding myself referred to . . ." Ibid., 271.

p. 76, "was the only subject . . ." O'Reilly, *Girl*, xii.

p. 76, "I began to grasp . . ." Ibid., xii.

p. 76, ". . . a friend of mine . . ." Ibid., 24.

p. 77, "On Fire Island . . ." Ibid., 25.

p. 77, "reading at random . . ." Mary Thom, ed. *Letters to Ms. 1972-1987* (New York: Henry Holt and Company, 1987,) xii.

p. 78, "reading the words of generous . . ." Ibid., xiii.

p. 79, "I remember her on the screen . . ." Steinem, *Outrageous Acts*, 233.

p. 80, "the neediness that so many . . ." Ibid., 233.

p. 81, "What I really want to say . . ." Ibid., 236.

p. 81, "I'll give it six months . . ." "*Ms.* Herstory," 2.

p. 81, "C-sharp on an untuned piano . . ." Ibid., 2.

Chapter Ten: Trashing

p. 83, "Mother Superior . . ." Heilbrun, *Education*, 242.

p. 83, "man-hating radicals." Ibid.

p. 84, "except where it is necessary . . ." *Roe v. Wade*, Supreme Court of the United States, 410 U.S. 113, January 22, 1973.

p. 86, "They looked at us like . . ." Sydney Ladensohn Stern. *Gloria Steinem: Her Passions, Politics, and Mystique*, (Secaucus, N.J.: Birch Lane Press, Carol Publishing Group, 1997,) 282.

p. 87, "tell them that this . . ." Steinem, *Outrageous Acts*, 143.

p. 88, "Gloria Steinem has a ten-year . . ." Susan Brownmiller, *In Our Time: A Memoir of Revolution*, (New York: The Dial Press, Random House, Inc., 1990,) 255.

p. 89, "I took no orders . . ." Ibid., 241.

p. 89, "the *Ms.* Myth . . ." Ibid., 292.

Chapter Eleven: Revolution from Within

p. 91, "I believed so little . . ." Steinem, *Revolution*, 6.

p. 91, "While she was alive . . ." Heilbrun, *Education,* 343.

p. 92, "seemed already to exist . . ." Ibid., 344.

p. 93, "Isn't this interesting." Ibid. 377.

p. 96, "She feels relaxed . . ." Steinem, *Revolution*, 159.

p. 96, "It was odd to discover . . ." Ibid., 160.

p. 97, "I finally began to admit . . ." Heilbrun, *Education*, 392.

p. 97, "There is always one . . ." Steinem, *Revolution.* 323.

p. 97, "a shadowed forest . . ." Ibid., 263.

p. 97, "I was going to live . . ." Ibid., 243.

p. 97, ". . . a friend sent me a photograph . . ." Claudia Dreifus, "*Ms*.behavin' again," *Modern Maturity*, May/June 1999. AARP Webplace, www.aarp.org/mmaturity/may_jun99/interview.html. 5.

p. 98, "What I remember most . . ." Steinem, *Moving,* 256.

p. 98, "We're calling it a 'partnership'. . ." Lorraine Ahearn, "Gloria Steinem's Hopeful Words: 'Just Married'," *Greensboro* (NC) *News & Record*, Sept. 15, 2000.

p. 98, "Thirty years of the women's movement . . ." Steinem. Author's correspondence, June 16, 2001.

p. 99, "I'm happy, surprised . . ." "People in the News," *Greensboro News & Record*, September 6, 2000.

Bibliography

Books and Articles:

Ahearn, Lorraine. "Gloria Steinem's Hopeful Words: 'Just Married'," Greensboro *News & Record*, Sept. 15, 2000.

Brownmiller, Susan. *In Our Time: A Memoir of a Revolution.* The Dial Press, Random House, Inc., New York, 1999.

Heilbrun, Carolyn G. *The Education of a Woman: The Life of Gloria Steinem.* The Dial Press, Bantam Doubleday Dell Publishing Group, New York, 1995

O'Reilly, Jane. *The Girl I Left Behind: The Housewife's Moment of Truth and Other Feminist Ravings.* Macmillan Publishing Co., Inc., New York, 1980.

Steinem, Gloria. *Moving Beyond Words.* Simon & Schuster, New York, 1994.

———. *Outrageous Acts and Everyday Rebellions.* Holt, Rhinehart and Winston, New York, 1983.

———. *Revolution from Within: A Book of Self-Esteem.* Little, Brown and Company, Boston, 1992

Stern, Sydney Ladensohn. *Gloria Steinem: Her Passions, Politics, and Mystique.* Birch Lane Press, Carol Publishing Group, Secaucus, N.J., 1997.

Thom, Mary, ed. *Letters to* Ms. *1972-1987.* Henry Holt and Company, New York, 1987.

Internet:

Bellafante, Ginia. "Feminism: It's All About ME!," *Time.com*, http://www.time.com/time/magazine/1998/dom/980629/cover1.html, June 29, 1998.

Dreifus, Claudia. "*Ms.*behavin' again," *Modern Maturity*, http://www.aarp.org/mmaturity/may_jun99/interview.html, May/June, 1999.

Flanders, Laura. "The 'Stolen Feminism' Hoax: Anti-Feminist Attack Based on Error-Filled Anecdotes," *EXTRA!*, Fairness and Accuracy in Reporting (FAIR), http://www.inform.umd.edu/EdRes;Topic/Wom...gRoom/AcademicPapers/stolen/feminism/hoax, Sept./Oct., 1994.

George, Don. "Gloria Steinem - On the Web," Ms. Foundation for Women and GNN, http://www.sherryart.com/daughters/daughters/gloria.html, April 25, 1996.

"Ms. Herstory" *Ms.*, http://www.msmagazine.com/msherstory.html, 2000.

"Some Basic Concepts of Theosophy: An Overview and Resources for Independent Study," Theosophical University Press, http://members.aol.com/tstec/hmpage/tsideas.htm, 2000.

Sommers, Christine Hoff. "Feminist Fatale," *The New Criterion on-line*, wysiwyg://16/http://www.newcriterion.com/archive/14/oct95/sommers.htm, Oct. 1995.

Steinem, Gloria. "What It Would Be Like If Women Win," *Time* Capsule, *Time* Education Program, http://www.time.com/time/teach/archive/000424/text5.html, Aug. 31, 1970.

Van Gelder, Lindsy. "Chronicle and Crucible," *The Nation Digital Edition*, http://www.thenation.com/issue970811/0811.vang.htm, Aug. 11-18, 1997.

"Who's Come A Long Way, Baby?," *Time* Archives. http://www.time.com/time/magazine/1998/dom/980629/ cover_related.html, Aug. 31, 1970.

Author's Correspondence:
Steinem, Gloria. November 28, 2000, and June 16, 2001.

Index

Abzug, Bella, *57*, 69, *71*
"After Black Power,
    Women's Liberation," 61
American Theosophical Society, 12

Bale, David, 98
Breakfast at Tiffany's, 41
Brownmiller, Susan, 69

Capote, Truman, 36, 41
Carbine, Patricia, 86, 93
Central Intelligence Agency
    (C.I.A.), 34, 88
Chávez, César, 49-51, 56, 58
Chisholm, Shirley, 69
"Click! The Housewife's Moment of Truth," 76-77
Communist Youth Conference, 34, 88
Cooke, Alistair, 26
Council on Women, 12

"Dissension Among Feminists," 89
Doe v. Bolton, 79
Dylan, Bob, 32

Eagle Forum, 89
Equal Rights Amendment
    (ERA), 67, 75, 84-85, 89
Esquire, 36-37, 44

Falwell, Jerry, 92
Federal Bureau of Investigation (FBI), 87-88
Feigen, Brenda, 67, 69
Felker, Clay, 37, 49, 72, 73
The Feminine Mystique, 40
Ford Foundation, 90
Freidan, Betty, 40, 42, 48, 66, 69-70, 72, 83

Gandhi, Mahatma, 29, 31
Gandhians, 29-30, 86
Graham, Katherine, 73, 90

Heffner, Hugh, 41, 45
Help! For Tired Minds, 38
House Un-American Activities Committee, 80
Hughes, Dorothy Pittman, 74

"I Was a Playboy Bunny," 45, 92
"If Men Could Menstruate," 92
"In Praise of Women's Bodies," 92
Independent Research Service, 34, 88
Indian Tourist Bureau, 28

Kennedy, Flo, 63, 74
Kilpatrick, James J., 81
King, Martin Luther, Jr., 31-32, 49
Kurtzman, Harvey, 38

League of Women Voters, 69
Liberty Media for Women, 98
Life, 50

Mad, 38
McCall's, 81, 86
McCarthy, Eugene, 47
McGovern, George, 47-48, 55-56, *57*, 79
Monroe, Marilyn, 79-81
Moral Majority, 92
Moses, Marion, 50, 52, 56, 58
Ms. Foundation for Women, 82

Ms., 73-79, 81-82, 85-95, 97-98

National Organization for Women (NOW), 48, 61, 67
National Press Club, 82
National Women's Political Caucus (NWPC), 69, *71*, 75
Nessim, Barbara, 37
New York Post, 90
New York Times, 87, 89
New York, 37, 49, 59, 61, 72-73
Newsweek, 62, 65-66
Nichols, Mike, 46
1975 International Women's Year Conference, 89
1977 National Women's Conference, 89
Nixon, Richard, 79
Nuneviller, Marie Ochs, 9-10, 12

O'Reilly, Jane, 76
Outrageous Acts and Everyday Rebellions, 9, 92

People, 86
Playboy Club, 41, 45
Playboy, 41

Reagan, Ronald, 90

Reasoner, Harry, 81
Redstockings, 58, 88-89
*Revolution from Within: A
    Book on Self Esteem*, 96
Roe v. Wade, 79, 84
"Ruth's Story," 92

Schlafly, Phyllis, 89
Show, 36, 41-42
Sloan, Margaret, 74
Smith College, 18, 23, 25-26,
    42
Steinem, Gloria,
    abortion, 27-28, 59
    breast cancer, 93
    childhood, 14-18, 20-24
    dancer, 21-22
    education, 16, 23-27
    and George McGovern,
        47-48, 55-56, 79
    India, 28-30
    and Independent Research
        Center, 34-35, 87-89
    legacy, 99
    marriage, 27, 46, 98
    Ms., 67-68, 72-78, 79-81,
        84-87, 89-94, 97-98
    as Playboy Bunny, 41-42,
        44-45
    public-speaking, 63-64,
        68, 74, 82, 99
    and United Farm Work-
        ers, 50, 52, 56, 58
    as writer, 28, 33, 35-38,

        44-45, 49, 61-62, 65-
        66, 79-81, 87, 91-92,
        96
Steinem, Leo, 9-10, *11*, 12-
    18, 20-21, 23-24, 37, 39
Steinem, Pauline, 12
Steinem, Ruth, 9-10, *11*, 12-
    18, 20-26, 33, 83-84, 87,
    91-92
Steinem, Susanne, 13-16, 18,
    20, 23-26, 33, 37, 87, 91
Susskind, David, 66-67

Time, 50, 65-66
Today, 50
Toledo Blade, 13

United States Supreme Court,
    78-79, 84
University of Toledo, 10, 12

Van Gelder, Lindsy, 72
Voters for Choice, 98

Washington Post, 73, 89-90
Watergate Scandal, 84
"We Have Had Abortions,"
    76
"What It Would Be Like If
    Women Win," 65-66
Wolfe, Tom, 39
"The Woman Who Died Too
    Young," 80, 92
Women's Action Alliance,
    67, 69